businessbuddies

successful
negotiating

D1316605

businessbuddies

successful
negotiating

Ken Lawson, M.A., Ed.M.

BARRON'S

First edition for the United States, its territories and dependencies, and Canada
published 2006 by Barron's Educational Series, Inc.

Conceived and created by
Axis Publishing Limited
8c Accommodation Road
London NW11 8ED
www.axispublishing.co.uk

Creative Director: Siân Keogh
Editorial Director: Anne Yelland
Design: Sean Keogh, Simon de Lotz
Managing Editor: Conor Kilgallon
Production: Jo Ryan, Cécile Lerbiere

NOTE: The opinions and advice expressed in this book are intended as a guide only. The publisher
and author accept no responsibility for any loss sustained as a result of using this book.

All inquiries should be addressed to:
Barron's Educational Series, Inc.
250 Wireless Boulevard
Hauppauge, New York 11788
www.barronseduc.com

Library of Congress Control No: 2005921779

ISBN-13: 978-0-7641-3245-2
ISBN-10: 0-7641-3245-8

Printed and bound in China
9 8 7 6 5 4 3 2 1

contents

Introduction

A famous *Rolling Stones* song reminds us time and again that "You can't always get what you want/But if you try sometime, you'll find you get what you need." The words are all too true to life. It's rare to get everything you could possibly want and much more common to have to settle for just a portion of what you desire, however large or small. In a business environment, with its churning dynamic of commercial thrust, strong personalities, and intense competition, compromise is almost always the order of the day. So what is it that enables motivated, planful individuals to achieve more of what they want, rather than less?

The answer has to do with a phenomenon that's treated thoroughly and creatively in the pages of this book: Negotiation. Simply put, negotiation is the strategic process of give and take that, when successfully executed, enables you to get what you need. Once you hone your negotiating skills you will find that it is possible to get not only what you need, but more, too.

Is negotiation a dirty word? Does it refer to an underhanded activity, or a knack for coercion that's developed and practiced by devious characters with selfish motives? In a word, no. In many people's minds, negotiation is a shady process to be avoided by people of integrity and by people who are content with what life puts in their path. But in another very real sense, negotiation is a skill that enables thoughtful, talented individuals to expand their experience and achieve more of what's available to them.

In *Successful Negotiating*, several distinctive negotiating styles are described and guides are offered to help you understand how they work. Armed with this insight, you'll understand which style is right for you to use in key negotiations of your own—and gain a heads-up about tactics you may experience on the receiving end.

You'll learn why preparation for the negotiation process is critical to its outcome, and how best to go about it. The book shows you how to bring

Introduction continued

sharp critical thinking to your preparation so that you can formulate a clear vision of your hoped-for outcomes and execute compelling strategies for attaining them. You'll learn how to develop a big-picture game plan and a persuasive agenda. And you'll understand why your success may hinge on a critical tool that experienced negotiators never leave home without: The BATNA.

Successful Negotiating is an indispensable toolbox that's filled with ideas, insights, and guidelines on managing the negotiation process in almost any challenging setting. You'll learn how to mingle objectivity with subjectivity to view and evaluate what's on the table; how to frame thoughts and concepts to your negotiating advantage; how to read and use body language to gauge the dynamic of the negotiation dialogue; and how to ask questions that get pointed answers—and results.

Finally, you'll learn how to respond when the negotiation process gets derailed. The book provides a host of "minefield" scenarios that show how missteps can undermine the negotiation process and sabotage the achievement of your cherished goals. You'll learn how to spot danger signs in the road, and navigate your negotiation vehicle around them.

Above all, *Successful Negotiating* is an engaging read for motivated individuals. It will empower you to take initiative, to take control, and to take the lead in just about any negotiation process. It's a valuable guidebook that can help you claim all of what you need—and lots more of what you really want.

Ken Lawson, M.A., Ed.M.
Career management counselor and author
Instructor, School of Continuing and Professional Studies
New York University

what is negotiating?

Processes, aims, and outcomes

A negotiation is a process that is intended to produce an agreement. It does not matter whether you are negotiating the sale of a house, a multibillion dollar corporate merger, or a divorce, the techniques are the same.

THESE ARE SOME DEFINING CHARACTERISTICS OF A SUCCESSFUL NEGOTIATION:

1 Negotiation is a process, not an outcome. Negotiating parties are often unwilling to move from their stated positions when they feel that an outcome is not forthcoming quickly enough, or that it won't be enough of a victory for them. This misses the point: Skilled negotiators judge a negotiation on how well the process of reaching an agreement is coming along.

2 A skillfully negotiated agreement provides mutual satisfaction—a "win-win" situation. Although it is possible for one more powerful side to exercise its greater muscle over a less powerful opponent, the agreement will rarely hold—the less powerful side will be resentful and will seek ways of reversing the agreement or not fulfilling its terms, resulting in mutual dissatisfaction.

3 Everything is negotiable. This means that all the terms of any prospective deal, the environment in which the negotiation takes place, even the personnel involved in the negotiation are changeable and subject to alteration. Do not believe any opponent who tells you "this deal is nonnegotiable."

4 Concessions are the currency of negotiation. If you just agree to what you are being offered, you may end up with a quiet life, but it is almost certain that you are not getting the best deal. Look for concessions from your opponent, and, in return, be prepared to give, or at least look as though you are giving, concessions to your opponent. Concede on minor issues in order to reach agreement on major ones.

Negotiating styles

All negotiators are people. This is important to realize, but it is often overlooked. Negotiators are not machines or computers. This means that there are as many different styles of negotiator as there are people. However, below is a breakdown of the broad categories that most negotiators fall into.

1 "HARD TACTIC" NEGOTIATORS

Hard tactic negotiators will typically:

- Seek victory at all costs.
- Demand concessions.
- Adopt one position from which they are unwilling to move.
- Distrust everything they are told.

2 "SOFT TACTIC" NEGOTIATORS

Soft tactic negotiators want to be friends with their opponents, and will typically:

- Avoid confrontation.
- Make concessions in order to foster friendship.
- Change their minds often.
- Take statements on face value.

3 **"ANALYZER" NEGOTIATORS**

Analyzer negotiators seek to control the process and typically:

- Demand facts and figures to back up all statements.
- Consider negotiations to be a game of chess.
- Disregard emotional elements.
- Ruthlessly apply logic and rationality.

4 **"CONSENSUS" NEGOTIATORS**

Consensus negotiators conduct what Fisher and Ury (*Getting to Yes*, 1981) call "principled negotiations." They typically:

- Seek to create rapport.
- Look for agreements that create mutual satisfaction.
- Listen to their opponents' concerns.
- Focus on interests, not positions.

Negotiating styles continued

The first two types of negotiator are at opposite ends of the spectrum. The analyzer is also likely to be a hard-style negotiator, though not as hard as the hard tactic negotiator. The consensus negotiator is likely to be a soft-style negotiator, though not as soft as the soft tactic negotiator.

In a room full of people with a variety of styles, there is always the possibility of a clash of styles. The hard negotiator will quickly become tired of the nice negotiator's friendly tactics, and the consensus negotiator will be frustrated with the analyzer's one-dimensional approach. These clashes can lead to a breakdown in negotiation before any substantive issues are discussed.

In short, people issues, that is, issues relating to a combination of human nature and negotiating styles, overshadow negotiation issues, and learning how to separate the two, and direct the negotiation away from personality and style clashes and toward finding a mutually beneficial agreement is an important skill.

It is very helpful to look at your own style, based on the descriptions above, and decide which one best describes you, and which ones best describe your colleagues and negotiation partners. In doing so, you will be able to understand better why they behave in the way that they do, what their motivations are, and how to head them off.

The important thing to avoid with clashes in negotiating style is the temptation to think that only one style will win out in the end. Simply pushing for everything you can get while being determined to give nothing away will produce little in the way of productive discussions and agreements. Conversely, being nice to everyone in the hope that appealing to everyone's better nature will get you what you want is unlikely to produce the best results either. This means that you should be prepared to adapt your style to the circumstances—a degree of flexibility is essential.

what is negotiating?

Coercion, manipulation, and persuasion

Typically, negotiators attempt to get their opponents to agree to their wishes using three methods: coercion, manipulation, and persuasion. Your opponent may use all three at once or switch among them, depending on how well each one is working. Of course, you are free to employ the same tactics.

COERCION

This type of powerplay assumes that one side is more powerful than the other, and that the stronger side will use its superior power to bend the weaker side to its will. Any agreement will be biased in favor of the stronger party. The stronger party will often coerce the weaker party into making a one-sided agreement by making it aware of the punitive consequences of not agreeing to its demands.

MANIPULATION

Most skilled negotiators realize that coercing an opponent into a one-sided agreement is not productive in the long term. An opponent will generally attempt to wriggle out of any obligations that are detrimental to her own interest. To make the negotiation more palatable, one side may attempt to dupe her opponent into agreement with manipulation tactics. These include: bluffing, selectively disclosing information, presenting information in a misleading way, practicing some forms of deception, and issuing last-minute ultimatums, to name but a few.

PERSUASION

Persuasion is something you do *with* an opponent, not *to* an opponent. It is more dependent on principled negotiations, and is based on facts, hard data, fairness, reason, principle, accurate disclosure, and skilled communication, not bullying or trickery. Because persuasion takes much practice, it is often bypassed by less skilled negotiators. Those who have mastered the art, though, usually unmask their bullying counterparts easily, and can form long-term, mutually beneficial working relationships with their opponents.

Aiming for mutual satisfaction

Too often in negotiations, it is assumed there is only one pie, of a fixed size, to be divided up. The parties lock horns, and whoever gets the most pieces is the victor. Skillful negotiators do not look at issues this way.

SO, TO START:

1 The pie is not a fixed size, and it is even possible for both parties to have joint ownership of individual pieces, if this leads to mutual long-term benefit.

2 To achieve this, you have to find shared interests. Deciding on your own interests, your opponent's interests, and where the two overlap to produce a shared interest is a key starting point in any negotiation. This can be applied to any business situation, from negotiating a pay raise following a promotion to agreeing a complex corporate merger.

The key idea here is that both sides have to work toward finding shared interests—which may not be immediately obvious. However, by explicitly stating that you wish to move toward finding shared goals, you will be able to exert influence over the discussion. This will mark you out as someone who is not just attempting to put one over on the opposition.

EXAMPLE
A shopkeeper interested in maximizing her profits overcharges her customers, who feel cheated, refuse to go back to the shop again, and may even discourage others from shopping there. Both sides lose. If, however, the shopkeeper charges her customers fairly, her short-term profits may be reduced, but shared interests will lead to a profitable long-term relationship with a growing number of customers. So it is possible for both parties to win, even when their interests appear to be at odds with each other.

preparing to negotiate

preparing to negotiate

Doing your homework

No negotiator who is hoping to get the result he wants will go into a meeting without gathering as much information on his opponent as possible. This is similar to police gathering intelligence before deciding what action to take. Simply going into a meeting armed with nothing more than high hopes will result in disappointment.

THESE ARE THE ISSUES YOU WILL NEED TO DO YOUR HOMEWORK ON:

1 YOUR OPPONENT'S INTERESTS

Knowing what your opponent wants from the negotiation in terms of the outcomes that he is looking for is essential. This will help you gauge what his most important demands will be, where he is likely to make concessions, and how you should pitch your demands in return.

2 YOUR OPPONENT'S NEGOTIATION STYLE

As mentioned on pp. 14–17, it is important to quickly recognize your opponent's style. This will help you determine what his hot buttons are likely to be, when and why he may become impatient, and the methods he may use to reach an agreement with you. Knowing how to lead your opponent around to your way of thinking by not reacting to the way in which he behaves is a key factor in skillful negotiations.

3 THE TACTICS AND PLOYS YOUR OPPONENT IS LIKELY TO USE
Will your opponent use underhanded tricks to get his way? Research all the tricks that he is likely to use, be prepared to spot them, and deal with them.

4 THE BARGAINING STRENGTH OF YOUR OPPONENT
Who are you dealing with, and what type of company does he represent? A large company will seemingly have greater bargaining strength than a smaller one.

Doing your homework continued

5 **YOUR OPPONENT'S TIME AND EFFORT**
Knowing how many resources your opponent can spare for the negotiation is very valuable information. For example, you may be able to reach an agreement more favorable to your own supply company if you know that your opponent is under serious time pressure to reach an agreement with a supplier of parts for a particular product.

6 **THE IMPORTANCE OF A FAVORABLE OUTCOME TO YOUR OPPONENT**
Does your opponent need to do business with you? Or are there many other companies like yours that could supply your opponent with the same goods? You will need strategies to convince your opponent that your company will best suit his long-term needs, while also not conceding too much in the short term.

7 **YOUR OPPONENT'S STATUS**
Who will you be meeting with? Some companies will attempt to intimidate you by sending powerful company directors to negotiate with you. Similarly, deliberately intimidating or unsettling environments can also play a part in the powerplay.

8 YOUR OPPONENT'S FINANCIAL SITUATION
Be careful how you interpret this one. Rich companies, usually those with a monopoly, can often be lazy in striking a good deal, but they may also be rich because they strike great deals. The reverse is true for companies operating on a shoestring, or in financial difficulty—they may be desperate to do any kind of business at all, or be only willing to pay next to nothing. Check your opponent's financial history, and his reputation for driving hard bargains.

9 THE TYPE AND SIZE OF YOUR OPPONENT'S COMPETITORS
Get a clear view of the wider industry picture, and see how your opponent is positioned within that industry. If he is attempting to break into that industry, he may be more likely to operate on lower profit margins in the short term in return for market penetration, which you can turn to your advantage. More established companies may be less flexible.

Positions vs. interests

Commonly, negotiations break down because the protagonists adopt a position, and then stick to it. The more pressure each side applies in order to force an agreement, the more entrenched those positions become.

In short, no agreement is likely if you are simply defending a given position. To break this cycle, it is imperative to look behind your opponent's position to see why he adopted it in the first place. These motivations are always driven by your opponent's interests. Interests are composed of needs and desires.

The skillful negotiator will always try to find where the interests of the other party lies. This means finding out and acknowledging the forces that are driving him. Gaining this knowledge is the basic starting point in reaching any agreement. And in any negotiation, there will always be driving interests, even if on the surface, the positions of both parties appear poles apart. Consider the following example.

ENTRENCHED POSITION

A real estate owner decides to sell some of his company's assets. He sets a purchase price of $300,000 for the property he is selling. The buyer, who is intending to rent out the property, may only be prepared to pay $250,000.

The seller is adamant that he will not lower the price, and the buyer refuses to increase his offer.

On the face of it, there is no chance of reaching agreement here—the two parties' positions are too far apart. In fact, the more they react to each other's positions, the more entrenched their own become and the less likely it is that they will take the time to discover each other's motivating factors.

Positions vs. interests continued

EXPLORING MOTIVATION

A close look at the interests behind the positions of both parties shows that there may be room for maneuver. By exploring the seller's motivations, the buyer discovers that the seller is charging $300,000 because his real estate company has large debts to pay off over the coming year. His interest lies not so much in the actual money, but in not living with constant financial worry. The seller explores the buyer's motivations and finds out that the buyer has set himself a limit of $250,000, not because he cannot afford any more, but because his calculations show that rental income on this property will not stretch to cover the mortgage needed to meet the $300,000 purchase price. His interest lies not so much in the actual money, but in not making a loss on his investment.

OPENING UP POSSIBILITIES

The two parties now have something to discuss. If the buyer can promise the seller a quick purchase and a large, up-front cash deposit, the seller will be able to pay off his debts immediately, rather than over a longer time period. This gives him the peace of mind to drop the price.

The seller can show the buyer that the luxury improvements he has made to the house will attract a higher rent than normal for houses in the area, he can prove that the property is worth the extra expense. So now there is the potential for an agreement, where previously there was none.

Bear in mind that the buyer and seller may still not reach agreement. However, finding out about each other's motivating interests means that agreement is now more likely.

preparing to negotiate

Finding out about interests

So how do you go about discovering the other party's interests? The only way is to ask key questions.

SCENARIO
You are the manufacturer of auto parts, which you deliver to a large chain of garages on a regular basis. Your contract is up for renewal. Your opponent unexpectedly asks that the parts be delivered much faster than usual, a demand that you cannot meet, but your opponent is adamant. Of course, you do not want to lose the contract. The temptation is simply to argue backward and forward, with both sides defending their positions. To avoid this, address these key issues:

1

WHY IS YOUR OPPONENT IS SO INSISTENT?
It may transpire that his warehouse cannot take delivery at the normal time, so he needs to bring the date forward. So the interest you may then seek to serve becomes warehouse space, not delivery dates.

2 WHAT WILL BE THE IMPACT ON HIM OF YOUR SUGGESTIONS
OR CONCESSIONS?
This will help you quickly understand what is motivating him,
but it also means you must decide on the consequences of your
suggestions and concessions. Skillful negotiators will try to:

■ Maximize the impact on their opponent's interests
■ Minimize the cost to their own side

Ask if you can make alternative delivery arrangements that
would get around the warehousing problem and allow you
to deliver the parts at the normal time. This would have a
high impact on your opponent's interests (and yours) at little
cost to you.

3 HOW MANY INTERESTS DOES YOUR OPPONENT HAVE?
On the face of it, he has only one interest—getting his auto parts early to avoid a log jam at his warehouse. But you need to look beyond this immediate interest.

This means not just looking at the number of demands your opponent is making, but also the number of other people outside of the negotiation who may be affected by your opponent's decisions:

■ He has to consider the interests of other buyers working at his company who may be ordering supplies of their own to be delivered to the warehouse.

■ He has to consider the interests of other suppliers who may have contractual delivery dates that he cannot renegotiate.

■ He has to consider the interests of management–worker relations at the company. There is a history of labor disputes that always reignite when the warehouse is overstretched.

4

WHAT IS THE NATURE OF YOUR OPPONENT'S INTERESTS?
It is very easy to assume that the only interest large
corporations have is profit, or that political leaders' only interest
is power. By asking, you will avoid making damaging
assumptions. These are all examples of powerful interests:

- Well-being (physical, emotional, and financial)
- Recognition
- Equal or fair treatment
- Respect for principles or ethics are all powerful interests
- Money

In the auto parts scenario, you might have assumed the issue
was money—the company wanted a quick delivery to speed up
production and ultimately, sales. But simple logistics, not
money, was the real issue.

Adopting the right frame of mind

Developing and maintaining the right frame of mind is an essential skill in successful negotiating. The common belief is that negotiating is a game of chess that can be strategically played and rationally worked out against a set of objective criteria, leading to the successful attainment of a goal.

All these points have their place, but they miss one of the fundamental aspects of negotiating—all negotiations are carried out by humans.

To adopt the right frame of mind, you need to:

■ Relate
■ Interpret
■ Think flexibly

RELATE

You need to to relate to your opponent as a way of influencing the outcome of the negotiation. In short, you need to develop a relationship with your opponent that goes beyond focusing on the eventual outcomes you wish to see.

This does not mean that you should lose sight of your goals, but along the way, particularly in a lengthy negotiation, the way in which you are progressing should at least be as important as ticking the boxes on your list of demands.

INTERPRET

As the negotiation progresses, place a priority on interpreting how your opponent is thinking, and what his reactions are to your requests and concessions. This will enable to you to have a better chance of probing and responding to his interests. By doing so, you will have a much better chance of advancing your own interests—you will find common interests where none appeared at first.

THINK FLEXIBLY

Adopting a flexible frame of mind helps you to appreciate other people's motivations, fears, and concerns. This gives you a much greater chance of success than simply sticking to inflexible positions, viewing your opponent as an adversary to be overcome.

Further, by adopting a flexible frame of mind, it becomes possible to take the lead and direct the human influences that can get in the way of a successful outcome. Learning how to spot and manage these influences puts you in the driving seat.

Asking questions (I)

So asking questions is an essential component in any negotiation. You will need to have a wide range of questions ready to ask. These are the preliminary questions you will need to get answers to in order to decide how to proceed:

1 What do you need to achieve? Think about the outcomes and goals you are trying to attain.

2 What does your opponent need to achieve? You cannot hope to negotiate with someone if you do not know where he thinks the negotiation will be going.

3 What are the key issues for your opponent? This will help you gauge where the emphasis will lie. This information will enable you to see how your opponent's issues interact with your own.

4 What kind of relationship does your opponent want? This question relates to the human interaction aspect of your negotiation. Different opponents will be looking for and expecting different relations.

5 What are the long-term expectations of your negotiation? This question will determine whether your opponent is expecting the deal to be a one-shot, or whether it can lead to a long-term association. In the case of a long-term association, relationship-building becomes even more important.

6 What are the barriers to reaching a mutually beneficial agreement? This is a very complicated question that operates on several levels. It makes you think about not only the conflicts that may arise over different goals but also the issues surrounding negotiating styles, positions (and the interests behind them), and people and personality conflicts.

preparing to negotiate

What are your interests?

You also need to work out what your own interests are. Although this may sound obvious, it is not. You must remember to separate your position from the interests behind it. Before the meeting starts, therefore, you must consider the following three issues:

IDEAL

"Ideal" means that you must consider what you would, in an ideal world, most like to get out of your negotiation. These are the quotes, prices, schedules, deadlines, quality issues, and other hard factual data that form the backbone of the deal you are negotiating. However, don't forget the more human issues discussed previously. These may be building a relationship with a client or supplier by looking toward the medium- or long-term in terms of sacrificing short-term gain for slow-burn profitability. Alternatively, you may be looking for a quick, one-shot deal only. These points add up to what you "want."

CONTINGENCY

Unless your opponent is a complete pushover, or your interests dovetail neatly, you will have to prepare for the possibility that you may not get everything you want. In short, you will have to develop a contingency plan. This contingency plan should form what you "need," a point beyond which you cannot go on any of the main issues that make up your negotiation.

GOING-IN

The final issue to consider is your "going-in" price. This may be different from the price you want or the price you need and may be well above the price you want. It is a starting point from which you can shift in order to appear to give a concession if you need to. Ultimately, as long as you achieve your contingency price, you can do business (on the price issue, at least).

Thinking about assumptions

Asking questions means never assuming that you know what your opponent wants or needs. In fact, making assumptions is the enemy of successful negotiating. Assumptions mean dealing in inferences and value judgments rather than fact, and it is very easy to fall into the trap of making them.

You may be able to make some predictions on what your opponent's positions and interests are, but until you explore what those interests actually are, you will never really know. Many negotiations break down because assumptions are made that turn out to have no basis in fact, leaving the party who made the assumptions looking foolish.

The basis for this is evident in everyday life. The street-wise kid never takes anything for granted, never assumes his own safety, never assumes that anyone he meets has his best interests at heart, even when a person approaches him with a smile on his face. Instead he relies on his ability to make quick judgments based on fact and experience. Opposite is a list of questions the kid is likely to ask himself.

1 How is that person behaving toward me?

2 What is he saying?

3 What is his body language telling me?

4 Is there an escape route for me if I need to back out quickly?

5 Can I let the other person back down without losing face?

Thinking about assumptions continued

Your tactic in a negotiation should mimic the kid's approach, especially when dealing with a familiar opponent. It is easy to assume that his positions and interests never change, but they do. His seniority may have grown, his negotiating role may have changed, and his company's financial circumstances may have altered. You may assume that because he is from a similar background, you know how he will behave, or that because he is different in age, race, or gender, you do not expect to find much in common.

SKILLFUL NEGOTIATORS DO TWO THINGS TO AVOID MAKING ASSUMPTIONS, BOTH IN PREPARATION FOR, AND DURING, THE MEETING:

1

ASK, RATHER THAN TELL
In order to try to gain the upper hand in a negotiation, most people assertively tell their opponent what their interests and positions are in an attempt to "get in there" first and imply that this is the correct position from which to start. Skilled negotiators do not do this. Instead, they ask questions to check whether the conclusions they drew from information gathered prior to the meeting are actually correct.

2 LISTEN

Having asked these questions, skillful negotiators then take the time to listen to the answers they are given and to observe how the answers are given as well as what is being said. This is often called "active listening," and means taking listening past simply hearing and into the realm of the analytical, asking "What did that really mean?" or, "What was the tacit information conveyed?" We will return to this on pp. 94–99.

3 OBSERVE

Correctly interpreting the body language expressed as the answer is given also provides valuable clues as to your opponent's real interests. In short, pay close attention to the answers you are given—it is pointless to adopt a flexible, questioning approach if you gloss over the answers. We will look at body language in more detail on pp. 100–107.

Thinking about perceptions

Perceptions come under the same umbrella as assumptions, but they operate on a more emotional level. Perceptions exist in the mind, and they become a problem when no amount of objective data or fact can dispel them. This means that perceptions must be dealt with in their own right.

INEXPERIENCED NEGOTIATORS COMMONLY:

1

SEE THE MERITS OF ONLY THEIR OWN ARGUMENT
This is a powerful feeling that makes people see only what they want to see and to shut out (or focus on) the issues that confirm their perceptions. The danger here is that people's perceptions make them think that their issues are rightfully at the center of the negotiation and that their opponent's issues are of lesser importance and can be brushed away. When they find that their opponent will clearly not see things this way, they become defensive and entrenched.

2 ASSUME THE WORST

This is a common perceptual problem. The negotiator perceives that his opponent is out to demand an unfair agreement. He convinces himself that this is what the other side will actually do and acts accordingly, whether or not it was ever his opponent's intention. This perception leads down a dead end.

3 APPORTION BLAME

When things go wrong, the negotiator may attempt to use blame as a way of getting his own way. The other side, knowing that they will be held responsible, resists acknowledging any liability. In short, the negotiator will aggressively apportion blame while his opponent will become defensive and stubborn. Any chance for a negotiated solution is lost.

Thinking about perceptions continued

BY CONTRAST, SKILLED NEGOTIATORS COMMONLY:

1 UNDERSTAND THEIR OPPONENT'S POINT OF VIEW
This means not just appreciating that there are differences between two points of view, but actually feeling the opponent's predicament emotionally. A negotiator cannot fully understand his opponent's point of view unless this empathy is present.

2 UNDERSTAND THAT THEY CANNOT INFLUENCE OTHERS UNLESS THEY EMPATHIZE WITH THEM
The quickest way to influence people is to show that you care about their feelings. Then show how they might act differently while still having their basic interests satisfied. This is how the skilled negotiator can steer the discussion his way.

3 CHALLENGE PERCEPTIONS
This does not mean that the negotiator confronts his opponent and faces him down. Rather, it refers to an open and frank discussion, coming from both sides, on what perceptions need to be dispelled. It shows that each side takes the other seriously and will not dismiss each other's hopes and fears as unimportant.

4 USE SURPRISE
Nothing is more influential in changing perceptions than behaving in a way opposite to the one the opponent expects. If your opponent is expecting lack of cooperation, show how you can help meet his needs. If you have quarreled in the past, show how you would like to build bridges.

5 INVOLVE THEIR OPPONENT IN THE NEGOTIATED AGREEMENT
Most negotiators present their opponent with a *fait accompli*, with everything worked out in the negotiator's favor, save for a few concessions to make them look generous. No experienced negotiator will ever do this.

Including the other side in drafting proposals or contracts will automatically draw them onto your side by giving them a personal stake in reaching agreement. The process may be lengthy and concede a lot to the other side, but the effort is worth it—as we said at the start of this book, negotiation is a process, not an outcome.

The language of interests

We have seen that getting to the motivating factors behind your opponent's positions means searching out his interests by asking questions and testing assumptions. Searching out those interests and talking about them has its own language. Try these steps:

1 EXPLAIN WHAT YOUR INTERESTS ACTUALLY ARE
Say what you want—you cannot expect your opponent to guess. This deals with your opponent's assumptions about your interests, by answering his questions for him. It also helps you lead the negotiation.

For example, if your local council is planning to build a large overpass and local residents are concerned, state that you are concerned about the disruption the building work will cause to local businesses:

- The adverse effect that large trucks and road closures will have on traffic congestion.
- The eyesore that the overpass will create.
- The adverse impact on property values.

The council will not want to lose the vote of an angry local population during the next round of elections or get tied up by lawsuits, but these interests will not see the light of day unless they are communicated.

2 MAKE SURE THE FULL IMPACT OF YOUR INTERESTS IS FELT
State explicitly your interests (and theirs). It is no good saying that building the overpass will "create problems" and "the residents are unhappy" about it. Describe the full impact it will have on residents, traffic congestion, and local businesses, backed up with hard facts.

This gives your claims legitimacy, and legitimate interests are both convincing and difficult to ignore.

3 REMAIN FLEXIBLE IN YOUR OUTLOOK
Think about other ways of satisfying your interests. This means that you should retain a flexible approach to the range of solutions that best suit your interests. If you don't want the overpass built at all, you may be surprised to learn that the council has plans to put the new road through a tunnel. This serves your interests in not creating an eyesore and damaging property values, and serves the council's interests in still getting the road built.

The language of interests continued

4 ATTACK THE PROBLEM, NOT THE PEOPLE
This is a critical skill to learn when talking about interests.
Otherwise, all that will happen is the person you are speaking
to will become defensive and stop listening. Instead:

■ Explain the problems the road-building program will create
for the neighborhood.

■ Do not attack the councilors for making ill-conceived,
unacceptable decisions.

■ Commit yourself energetically to your interests—in this case
address the issues surrounding the council's decision to build
an overpass, and pursue your interest in solving the issues.

■ Support the person you are speaking to. This will further
reinforce the idea that you are not attacking him personally.

■ Thank him for his attention and time and show that you
understand his interests as well. This helps build a rapport
that will make solving the problem easier and quicker.

5 DEVELOP A PURPOSE IN YOUR LANGUAGE

Developing a purpose means that you need to have a clear idea of where you want the negotiation to go. This suggests that you need to:

■ Look forward and avoid point-scoring and entrenched positions and find a solution that mutually satisfies both sets of interests.

■ Not just react to what is said to you, which will set off a spiral of claim and counterclaim. Instead, listen and do not react.

■ Ask questions to find out why a particular position has been adopted; then see if there are any ways of satisfying your interests while still considering and understanding your opponents.

■ Find out why the overpass is necessary. What is the council's thinking behind it? What proposals do the council have for solving the difficulties the road-building will create?

This approach quickly gets to the heart of the matter—why the overpass is being built. But it avoids a dead-end scenario where you accuse the council of building an unnecessary road, and the council's counterclaim that it is necessary.

Developing an agenda

Before you go into any negotiation, you must know in advance what the issues to be discussed are. As with most meetings, it is best if you devise a formal agenda and share it in advance will all participants.

THE AGENDA SHOULD COMPRISE THE FOLLOWING BASIC ITEMS:

1

WHO WILL ATTEND
A quick list of those from all the parties, including their rank or job title, is useful information, particularly if not all the personnel have met each other before.

2

THE DURATION OF THE MEETING
A note to clarify how long the meeting will be will help all parties gauge how much detail the negotiation will go into. Assuming that no one will want to cut short an important discussion if you do run out of time, try to keep your schedule free in the period after the meeting to accommodate this possibility.

3 IF APPROPRIATE, WHO WILL START PROCEEDINGS

To keep both sides from jockeying for position, it is best that one side be nominated to start proceedings. This ensures that the meeting can proceed in a constructive fashion. You could also pencil in time for the other party to respond to the first party's opening.

4 THE ISSUES TO BE DISCUSSED

It is useful to list the main topics that are under discussion. This means only the main topics. If there is too much detail on side issues and peripheral negotiations, the point of the agenda is lost.

Developing an agenda continued

5 THE ORDER IN WHICH TOPICS WILL BE DISCUSSED
In addition to listing what the topics are, decide on the order in which they will be discussed. Consider:

- The natural order in which the topics need to be discussed in order to form a meaningful dialog.

- The relative importance of each.

Pay attention to getting this order right. An illogical agenda will quickly be discarded, which will harm your credibility.

6 THE TIME ALLOWED FOR EACH TOPIC
This ensures that you do not get bogged down on the first point and end up discussing nothing else throughout the meeting. Keep your eye on the clock to make sure that you stick to the time frame allocated, and that you are moving things along gently without appearing to be trying to control the meeting.
Say: "We have run out of time on this item. Can I suggest that we spend five minutes more on it and then move on?"

7 ISSUES THAT SHOULD NOT BE PART OF THE NEGOTIATION
This is particularly useful if you have a history of difficult
negotiations with your opponent. It will stop old issues from
being brought up again, particularly contentious ones. You
should not necessarily list these on the agenda itself, but
perhaps keep a side note for yourself of topics best avoided.

As with most aspects of preparing for a negotiation, having an agenda is not a recipe for guaranteed success in the meeting. It is, however, a good way of structuring your dialog so that you have the best possible chance of having a constructive discussion on the most important topics.

Developing an agenda continued

HOW TO DRAW UP A PREMEETING AGENDA:

1 Nominate one person to be the agenda coordinator. It becomes his responsibility to deal with the agenda and the parties to it.

2 You do not need a meeting about a meeting. Constructing an agenda can be done via email, phone, or fax.

3 Allow plenty of time to get the agenda together. Do not leave it until the last minute.

4 Contact all parties and ask for their agenda items. Place a limit on the number of items that can be put on the agenda.

5 Place a time limit on submissions for the agenda, but explain clearly what that time limit is.

6 Circulate the finished agenda to all parties shortly before the meeting. If appropriate, ask for revisions, but explain clearly that these must be kept to a minimum.

preparing to negotiate

Prioritizing your outcomes

Clearly, before you go into any negotiation, you must know what you want to reach agreement on. But it is not enough to have this information. You must also know which issues can be agreed quickly and carry the most weight, and which ones are less important.

THIS IS NOT JUST A QUESTION OF WRITING AN "I WANT" LIST WITH THE MOST IMPORTANT ITEMS AT THE TOP OF THE LIST. IT MEANS:

1 Checking your own interests (rather than positions).

2 Checking the interests of the other side (be prepared to be flexible on what these are and be open to the possibility that you are wrong).

3 Compiling the "proof" you need to back up your arguments, in terms of data, facts, and evidence.

These three factors will decide how much success you are likely to have with each of your key issues to be negotiated, and will help you rank them accordingly. This creates a list of ideal outcomes. You will be able to see where interests clash, where interests are shared, and how you will be able to back up your claims, or the evidence your opponent will use to back up his claims.

If there are many areas on which the parties clash, your ideal outcomes list will probably be quite modest—you will not be able to gain agreement in your favor when both parties are far apart in their interests. Conversely, where there are many shared interests, your ideal outcomes list will be more ambitious. With both parties pulling in the same direction, more can be agreed upon.

In the next section, we will look at what to do when your ideal outcomes do not come fruition, and you need a fallback position.

Fallback position—your BATNA

Despite all your homework and skilled negotiating techniques, you may not be able to reach agreement on your main issues. So what are you going to do? Go back to the office empty-handed, with no agreement? This is exactly what happens to inexperienced negotiators.

To avoid this, you need to develop your BATNA—your Best Alternative To a Negotiated Agreement, a term coined by Roger Fisher and William Ury in *Getting to Yes* (1981). This is your predetermined fallback position, should you find yourself in a position where you are not going to get agreement on your most important agenda items. It is an essential tool and is the difference between going into the meeting well-prepared and badly prepared.

MAIN POINTS FOR YOUR BATNA:

1 The implication of a BATNA is that it is a second-best solution to your problems. This is a misconception. Your BATNA is just a different set of solutions, which should take you very close to achieving your original interests. It is not therefore your bottom line. It is an imaginative solution to the threat of not coming to an agreement.

2 Rather than be second-best, your BATNA allows you to operate from a position of strength because you have Plan B up your sleeve should Plan A fail. This makes it a powerful negotiating tool because you have a strong alternative.

3 Your BATNA stops you from being too committed to reaching an agreement. Having no fallback position puts you under a great deal of pressure to reach agreement and may result in your agreeing to things you may come to regret, simply so that you don't walk away from the table empty-handed.

Fallback position—your BATNA continued

Examples of good uses of BATNAs exist in all walks of life. You may have been offered a new job at a salary of $40,000. You may desperately need this job because you have been unemployed for a while and have debts to pay off, but it is not your ideal job. You also know that someone at the company doing the same job is earning $50,000, and you think that you should be paid the same. You ask for $50,000, but this request is turned down. So what do you do?

You really only have two options if you have no BATNA. You can either accept the job as presented to you at $40,000, or you can decide that you are unhappy with being underpaid and would be better off elsewhere. By developing a BATNA, you might be able avoid this either-or predicament, and developing it in advance of your salary negotiation will stand you in good stead. You could suggest:

1 That you take the job for $40,000, but on condition that management agrees to a performance review in six months where your salary can be renegotiated. You know that you can do the job well, and that your natural enthusiasm for a new job will show you in a very good light when six months is up.

2 You have another job interview lined up next month. In fact, the sector in which you work is expanding and there are several possible opportunities for higher-paid employment. You do not need this particular job.

3 Your debts can be paid off by other means. Perhaps you are prepared to sell your house if necessary. You have also always wanted to travel the world. You can buy a smaller apartment, rent it out while you are away, invest some of the profit from the sale in stocks and shares and use the rest to pay off your debts and fund your trip. You don't need the job at all.

Whichever of these outcomes may be relevant for you, any of them could form the basis for a good BATNA, and so stop you from being forced into accepting an underpaid job or facing financial ruin. Because you have alternatives, some of which lead to full pay, others to debt clearance, you are in a much stronger position to bargain—you are no longer desperate to accept the job.

Fallback position—your BATNA continued

To start, the key task is to develop your BATNA in advance of the meeting. "Develop" is the key word here—your BATNA needs to be a considered and planned; unless you are brilliant at thinking on your feet, good alternatives are unlikely to just pop into your head when you most need them. To develop your BATNA, consider the following four things:

1
LIST THE THINGS YOU MIGHT DO IF YOU CANNOT REACH AGREEMENT
As in our example, consider your alternatives. This does not mean making a knee-jerk reaction. It means considering any other possible options that would satisfy your interests.

2
USE YOUR RESOURCES
Developing your BATNA may take time. Use the resources available to you to make sure that you have fully explored the options available to you. This is particularly useful when your opponent is stronger than you. Knowledge, experience, intelligence, money, time, and networks of people are all resources you should put into developing the best BATNA you can. Simply having a good idea is not enough.

3 GET REAL

You might have a list of a dozen different alternatives, or you may only have one. In either case, be realistic, neither too pessimistic nor too optimistic about the chances of success for each. So do your homework, working out figures and hard facts, so that you base your decisions on observable data. This is important—it stops your BATNA from being a mere fairy tale.

4 CHOOSE THE BEST ONE

Base your decision on the evidence you have gathered. It is tempting to choose the alternative you like the best but has the least chance of working out. So the key is to be as honest as you can with yourself and to make a choice against which you can judge any offer you are made. Remember, the better your BATNA, and the more likely it is that you can actually implement it, the less pressure you are under to accept any terms you don't like in the current deal.

Fallback position—your BATNA continued

USING YOUR BATNA

Your BATNA is primarily a tool for you to decide whether there is an attractive alternative to the deal you are being offered so that you do not necessarily have to accept an unfavorable offer. However, if you have a great BATNA, it is worth letting your opponent know.

LEVERAGE

This information will give you a great deal of leverage.

In our example above, the best BATNA might be that you have had another job offer from a rival company. What better leverage could you have than to tell the management who are offering you the $40,000 job that rival is prepared to pay you a higher salary? A salesman might have another customer on the line who is willing to pay a better price for the consignment of car parts he is trying to sell. A property developer might have an investment bank that is willing to lend money at a lower rate of interest than the bank he is currently dealing with.

DON'T BLUFF

The key is to let your opponent
know that you have a good
alternative—and that you intend
to see it through. Do not do this
as a bluff—this should be a
genuine statement that your
BATNA exists and that you are
prepared to turn to it if need be.
For example, you may bring a
lawyer to a meeting to suggest
that your BATNA is legal action, or
you may even chose to leave the
negotiation to impress on your
opponent that you have another
alternative—and are prepared to
implement it.

Preparing what to say

Once you have done your homework, you need to practice how you are going to get the meeting off to a good start.

THERE ARE TWO MAIN OPENING PLOYS IN ANY NEGOTIATION MEETING:

1 TACKLING THE CONTENTIOUS ISSUES FIRST
This is an aggressive way of opening the negotiation. You go in and place your cards on the table and start off by dealing with the biggest issues first.

ADVANTAGES:
It cuts to the chase: No small talk is needed, and the main issues are brought out into the open honestly, with no attempt to mask or disguise them among the many other issues that may need agreement. It may also save a lot of time in the long run. If the issues are very contentious, then there is no point agreeing on peripheral points if talks will break down later. It also gives your opponent no time to gather information about you and your interests and motivations and so may catch him by surprise.

Also, an aggressive opening may be appropriate if you know that it matches your opponent's negotiating style. Also do it if it fits with your own negotiating style.

DISADVANTAGES:

It is a risky way to proceed as it can appear confrontational; it puts your opponent on the back foot and may force him into simply stating his position on the issues in hand. This risks getting into the entrenched positions that you need to avoid if you are to find a mutually beneficial agreement. It may also put your opponent off because you come across as being too aggressive at the start, which does not augur well for the rest of the meeting.

Preparing what to say continued

2 DEALING WITH THE SMALL ISSUES FIRST
A tried and trusted way is to work toward "yes," building up the number of "yes's" as you go through the initial exchanges of the meeting. This creates a feeling that agreement is possible on all issues. Conversely, if a meeting opens with a series of "no" answers, agreement becomes increasingly unlikely.

ADVANTAGES:
Because negotiation is a process and not an outcome, pacing the meeting so that mutual trust and cooperation are developed is usually considered a better option. This means that you get to know your opponent, his style, and the type of agreement he is looking for. It also means that you can quietly go about the all-important business of information-gathering.

DISADVANTAGES:

There is no guarantee that approaching the meeting in a less aggressive way will mean that agreement will be reached on the important issues. Also, be careful that you are not the one being lined up for a fall. The goodwill soft-talk may be playing directly into your opponent's hands as he attempts to soften the blow of a big demand later on the negotiation. Also, be aware that your opponent will be using the gentle approach to gather the information he needs to decide how to proceed.

OPENING THE NEGOTIATION

Whatever option you decide to use, being the one to open the negotiation will often give you an advantage. Just like a tennis player's service game, it will be up to your opponent to react to your opening lines. Float some relatively unimportant ideas and use them to gauge your opponent's reaction. This will tell you much about where his sensitivities lie.

preparing to negotiate

Thinking about cultures

All countries have their own cultures, and there are also regional differences within countries, and even within organizations. It is therefore unwise to go into a meeting expecting your opponent to have the same values, mannerisms, priorities, or viewpoints as you. This can be misconstrued as arrogance and conceit, quickly leading to a breakdown in communication.

1 NATURE OF TIME
Conceptions of time differ greatly across the world. For example, many Asian cultures tend to see time as cyclical. This is reflected in their major religions, such as Hinduism and Buddhism, which emphasize the cyclical nature of birth and rebirth. Western cultures tend to regard time as linear; it is a point toward which you travel. Returning to points already discussed may therefore be a feature of dealing with Asian counterparts.

2 LENGTH OF TIME

In addition to the nature of time, many cultures have a very different conception of what constitutes a long time. This becomes clear when your opponent is asking for time to make decision. Length of time is often linked to the age of the culture. There is a marked difference between what is regarded as a long time in Australia, compared to that in India.

3 AUTHORITY

Some negotiators are ambassadors for their companies, even their countries. This means that they may be more than willing to negotiate on the matters in hand but must defer to higher authority for a final decision. This may make them seem lacking in authority, but a rigid hierarchical structure may be the norm.

Thinking about cultures continued

4 RELATIONSHIPS

Some cultures place a great deal of emphasis on the building of relationships rather than on how clever your arguments and factual evidence is. In short, they need to know that you are worth dealing with before they will deal with you. Many Asian cultures have strict rules of behavior and etiquette when it comes to social protocol, which, if flouted, can hinder progress in a negotiation.

5 COLLECTIVISM

Some cultures operate in tightly controlled groups in which strictly observed social protocols dominate negotiation and how agreements are reached. This can clash with individualist cultures, who are able to operate outside of such constraints and who cannot understand why considering the wishes of many other people within a group should interfere with striking a deal.

6 GENDER, AGE, AND SENIORITY

Many cultures value these three issues differently. In the West, we are at great pains to level the playing field and now describe bias on the basis of gender, age, race, or any other difference as discriminatory. Some cultures however, naturally defer to their elders so as to show them the proper respect; men and women may not be equal, but are seen to fulfill valuable specific roles; greater seniority means less accountability to those below you.

There are many more generalizations to be made, across a whole range of cultures, countries, and subjects, but the important point to remember is that no two countries are ever the same. To minimize disruption and avoid miscommunications, try:

Thinking about cultures continued

1 DOING YOUR HOMEWORK
Research where you are going and find out about local customs, greetings, negotiating styles, the structure of each day, and the role of your opponent. Also find out about social rules governing etiquette and procedure. This will stop you from blundering into the most obvious traps. Doing some research into topics that should be off the menu is another good idea, particularly when it comes to politics and religion.

2 LEARNING THE LANGUAGE
Nothing looks better than a visitor, especially from an English-speaking country, who has made the effort to learn some of the language of the country he is visiting. In particular, learn greetings and how to say thank you—this is always taken as a sign of respect.

3 MEETING IN A NEUTRAL PLACE

High-level negotiations are often best conducted on neutral ground. World leaders regularly do this—one set of high-level arms control talks between Reagan and Breshnev in the 1980s were held in Rekyavik, Iceland, for example.

Clearly, in the business context, it would be very unusual to have to go to these lengths to find neutral territory, but the principle remains: It is best to avoid one another's offices where possible, particularly when dealing with contentious issues.

Also choose somewhere appropriate. A restaurant or coffee shop may be neutral ground, but it will not be a good idea if it is very busy, too small, or dimly lit.

Thinking about cultures continued

4 PREPARING FOR FORMALITY
You can be almost certain that whoever you are dealing with will meet and greet you with a high degree of formality—no one meets a stranger under these circumstances with a relaxed "Hi, how are you," a clap on the back, and an arm around the shoulder. Many cultures would regard this as rude and disrespectful. If visiting a foreign country, watch what your host does, and try to mimic what they do.

5 ACCEPTING AND OFFERING GIFTS AND COURTESY
If you are given a gift, accept it with courtesy, but try not to be too effusive. If you think you are likely to be given a gift make sure you can reciprocate, either by bringing a suitable one with you or making some other show of generosity.

As a note of caution, make sure that your gift does not offend! In some cultures certain items, or the materials they are made out of, may cause offense. An example is the story of a negotiator who presented his Indian opponent with a leather bag. Because the cow is a holy animal in the Hindu religion, his gift backfired.

INTERORGANIZATIONAL CULTURE

We have dealt with culture clashes between different nationalities, but all these points can just as easily apply to cultures within countries, where geography, a myriad of different languages within the same border, or age-old regional tensions present their own problems.

Equally, these points apply to differences within, and between, organizations themselves. Some organizations are global entities—meeting with colleagues from different offices across the world to divide up a major worldwide project, for example, will require many cultural negotiation skills, even though everyone should automatically be pulling in the same direction.

Also, some organizations have flat management structures and no dress code; by contrast, others are hierarchical and rigid and have strict rules of behavior, applicable to all.

Again, do your homework before you meet your opponent. Getting the negotiation off to a good start by behaving and speaking in an appropriate way is a must.

Thinking about communication

Skillful negotiators are also expert communicators. It is almost impossible to influence the outcome of a meeting if you struggle to get your interests across clearly and in a manner that can be understood.

COMMUNICATING IS ABOUT:

1 EXPRESSING YOURSELF IN THE APPROPRIATE MANNER
This does not mean forcing the other side to listen to your position, your demands, or your grievances. Remember, you are trying to come to a mutually beneficial agreement, and this will not happen if you are bullying, aggressive, boorish, inaudible, sulky, or dismissive.

2 EXPRESSING YOURSELF AT THE APPROPRIATE TIME
Expressing yourself is as much about knowing when to be quiet as when to talk. Talking incessantly, constantly interrupting your opponent, and spitting out expressions of disgust, disbelief, or dismissal are all ways to guarantee a breakdown in communications. Instead, hear the other side out, and remain calm and attentive while waiting your turn to speak.

3 LISTENING TO THE OTHER SIDE
You must also really listen to what your opponent is saying. This is a critical communication skill, which will stand you in good stead in a variety of business (and life) situations. Although we all think that we listen to those around us, very little of what we are told actually sinks in.

Really taking notice of what you are being told is called "active" listening (see pp. 94–99). This means taking on board what your opponent has just said, and asking questions about it. This shows that you have heard and understood him and is a powerful tool for influencing the negotiation process because we all have a basic human need for acknowledgment.

Thinking about communication continued

SO WHAT ARE THE TYPES OF EXPRESSION YOU SHOULD BE USING?

1 SPEAK CLEARLY

This means talking to the other side in a way they can understand. Impressive debating techniques, effective manipulation of outside organizations such as the press, or setting out to impress third parties like your boss will simply irritate your opponent. Instead, talk to your opponent, and your opponent alone, in a way that he can understand and respect.

2 EXPLAIN RESULTS AND OUTCOMES

Explain what the impact of your opponent's suggestions and interests are going to be on you. You will influence the negotiation process a lot more if you say: "The price you are proposing will put me out of business." Don't say "You are deliberately trying to bankrupt me."

The first sentence explains the impact on you and provides food for thought—your opponent will realize that you can never agree to the proposed price. The second explains nothing and accuses the other side of trying to harm your business.

3 SAY WHAT YOU MEAN
This is an adjunct to speaking clearly. Say what you have to say to get your point of view across and leave it at that. There is always the temptation to try to clear up every minor point, to paper over every crack, or to right every perceived wrong. Don't. Think about what you are going to say and the impact it is going to have on your opponent at that time.

4 CONSIDER THE WHOLE NEGOTIATION
Also think about the impact communication is going to have on the negotiation as a whole. This doesn't mean that you should shirk from saying difficult things if the situation merits it, but it does mean that you should think about how to make your speech compact and accurate, and the ramifications for the negotiating process of deviating from the point.

preparing to negotiate

Knowing your own weaknesses

The flip side of finding out your opponent's strengths and weaknesses is to be aware of your own. Rest assured that your opponent will be trying to find your vulnerable areas, and—irrespective of how good a negotiator you think you are—you will have some.

THESE ARE SOME TIPS FOR PREPARING YOURSELF FOR THE MEETING, AND FOR GAINING SOME SELF-KNOWLEDGE:

1 Ask a professional consultant to put you through a personality test. It can be very revealing!

2 Talk to the people who know you best, such as trusted colleagues with whom you have worked on negotiations before (perhaps including your boss), your partner, even your children.

3 Which areas of your negotiation do you know least about? These are the areas that need special attention because they are the ones that are most likely to trip you up.

4 Know how much pressure you are likely to be put under. To this end, find out about the people you are likely to encounter. Find out:

■ How long they have been with their companies. This will indicate how knowledgeably and definitively they can talk about their company and its policies and procedures.

■ How much experience they have. Experienced negotiators may expect to win more concessions, but they are also more likely to look for areas of mutual benefit than a less experienced one.

■ How successful they have been over the course of their employment. This will indicate how well they know their subject area. Again, this may make them demanding but want to reach a deal.

■ How familiar are they with your area? An opponent who knows the area under negotiation very well is likely to ask more searching questions than one who doesn't.

5 If you get stuck, practice your escape route. Say: "I cannot answer that point right away. I will make a note of your inquiry and get back to you when head office confirms the figures." This is much better than trying to bluff your way out of it—you will contradict yourself at some point.

Game plan checklist

So just what information and attitudes do you take into the meeting with you? Here is a recap of the key issues:

1 Decide what your positions are and the interests that motivate each one.

2 Decide what your ideal outcome is and your contingency for each of your interests.

3 What emphasis do you need to put on the need to develop a relationship with your opponent?

4 What adaptations will you make to your negotiating style?

5 What tactics will you use to deal with your opponent's negotiating style?

6 What questions will you ask to deal with your assumptions?

7 Where will you and your opponent's interests overlap?

Game plan checklist continued

8 What kind of concessions are you prepared to make?

9 How will you use questions to lead the negotiation?

10 Do you have a clear agenda, agreed with your opponent?

11 Do you have a strong fallback position, your BATNA?

12 Do you know what your priorities are?

13 Have you prepared what you want to say?

14 Do you know how you are going to say it?

KEY QUESTIONS

3

in the meeting

Getting off to the right start

After you have done all your homework and preparation, how you conduct the negotiation is the next important task. This is the cutting edge—you have walked into the venue you have chosen, have greeted your opponent, and are ready to begin.

First off, do not let your thorough preparation go to your head. You may think that you know all there is to know about your opponent and her interests, but the thoroughness you have used to prepare must be carried on throughout the meeting itself.

A key skill to adopt right from the start is that of really listening to your opponent. Often called "active" listening, this important technique allows you to influence the negotiating process, since if you are using it and your opponent is not, you will be way ahead in understanding what it is that is needed to come to an agreement. Active listening means:

1 BEING ATTENTIVE TO EVERYTHING YOU ARE BEING TOLD
This means paying attention and really listening. It is very easy
just to glaze over and take in only a part of what is being said
or to listen to the bits you want to hear. When your opponent
starts speaking, stop talking, make eye contact, and start to
concentrate. Do not do anything else until you have heard
everything your opponent has to say on the issue.

2 NOT INTERRUPTING WHILE YOU ARE BEING TOLD
You cannot listen actively if you yourself are talking, especially if
you are interrupting what your opponent is saying. Active
listening means staying quiet until the other person has had
her say. This is harder to do than you might imagine. The
temptation to interject, particularly if your opponent has said
something controversial or provocative, can be very strong.

3 NOT JUMPING TO CONCLUSIONS OR MAKING QUICK JUDGMENTS
Hearing someone fully means not just listening to the words,
but listening without prejudice. All too often, you think you
are hearing someone out, but you are quietly dismissing what
she has to say as you go along. This is not active listening
because you are not actually listening at all but merely
comparing what your opponent has to say to your own fixed
viewpoint. Where no match occurs, you dismiss her argument.

4 ASKING QUESTIONS TO CLARIFY WHAT YOU HAVE JUST HEARD
Demonstrate that you are really listening by asking questions
to clarify points as they are raised. This is not the same as
interrupting. You are encouraging your opponent to explain her
interests further, allowing you to listen more actively.

5 SUMMARIZING WHAT YOU HAVE JUST HEARD
To make sure you fully understand all the points that have just been raised, and to avoid making any damaging assumptions, summarize the main points of what you have just heard. Say:

"We have discussed lots of issues here, some of which we are well on the way to agreeing to, others which need further discussion. Can I just be clear on where we stand?"

Take notes as the discussion progresses. These are very useful if the discussion is complex, and stop you from missing any vital information that you may not be able to retain by listening alone. Tell your opponent that you wish to do this—it will keep her from thinking that you are noting what she says to use as ammunition against her later.

Getting off to the right start continued

ACTIVE LISTENING THEREFORE SERVES THREE IMPORTANT PURPOSES:

1

IT SERVES YOUR OWN NEEDS
How can you respond accurately to your opponent's interests and proposals if you do not fully understand them? Too rarely in negotiations, particularly when no agreement is being reached on a difficult issue, do the parties listen and speak with purpose. One claim is met with another, neither side expects to be heard, and no agreement is reached.

2

IT SERVES YOUR OPPONENT'S NEED TO BE ACKNOWLEDGED
We all need to be listened to and taken seriously. How many times have you been expressing what you think, only to be cut short or scoffed at? The result is always the same—a breakdown in the discussion and no agreement. As soon as you listen to what are often very real concerns, it shows you are taking your opponent seriously.

3

IT ENCOURAGES BOTH SIDES TO STOP THINKING IN TERMS OF POSITIONS ONLY

These positions may be so far apart as to make agreement impossible. Both sides become less defensive when they learn that their points of view are being listened to. You understand the other side's problem and don't just restate your own position.

ACKNOWLEDGING AND AGREEING

An important point to recognize here is that acknowledging what your opponent has to say does not mean that you are agreeing with her. It merely means that you understand that she has a valid point of view. This opens up the possibility that there are other points of view to be considered— your own. Be careful not to fall into the trap of looking like you have come round to her way of thinking.

Body language

The way in which we come across is determined not only by what we say but how we behave while we are saying it, in terms of tone of voice and body language; these are the nonverbal communication signals. Body language is an essential component in the communication process and how you hold and adjust your body position during the meeting will give away much about what you really think.

THESE ARE THE CLASSIC BODY LANGUAGE SIGNALS:

1 OPEN POSTURE

An open posture indicates willingness to listen, an open mind, a lack of defensiveness, and, by implication, an indication of control and authority over the proceedings. Look for these open postures in your opponent:

■ Body is facing you square-on

■ Legs and arms are uncrossed

■ Palms are turned upward

■ Head is looking straight ahead

■ Body leans toward you

■ Lots of neutral eye contact

2 CLOSED POSTURE

By contrast, a closed posture is the opposite. It indicates defensiveness and an unwillingness to listen or change an opinion. Look for these closed postures:

■ Body faces away from you

■ Legs and arms are crossed

■ Hands are palm down and are hidden

■ Head points at the floor

■ Body leans away from you

■ No eye contact, or eyes look at the floor

Body language continued

3 CHANGES IN POSTURE

More important than the postures themselves are changes in posture. Unless the negotiation progresses on an even keel throughout, no posture ever remains the same. The contrast between one posture and another is often a good indicator of sudden agitation or concern on the one hand, or agreement and acceptance on the other. Look for these signals:

■ A sudden stiffening in posture. This indicates disagreement but can also be a sign of alert interest if accompanied by a move forward.

■ A sudden crossing or uncrossing of the arms and legs. Crossing indicates defensiveness; uncrossing indicates an open posture.

■ A sudden movement to the back of the chair accompanied by crossed arms. This indicates reluctance but can also be relaxed acceptance.

■ A nervous shift to sit on the edge of their chair. This indicates and anxiety.

■ Clenched fists. This indicates frustration and anger.

■ Diverted attention, away from you and to the floor or a point over your shoulder. This disengagement indicates a lack of interest.

■ A sharp intake of breath or a sigh. This indicates disagreement or reluctance.

4 CHANGES IN EXPRESSIONS

Accompanying postures will be changing facial expressions, the most important of which come from the eyes. Look for these signals, positive and negative:

■ Eye contact may break and dart about. This may be accompanied by a slight bowing of the head. This indicates a lack of honesty.

■ Eye contact may break and eyes may stare into the middle distance. This indicates lack of interest.

■ An open, receptive face may quickly become closed and tense around the forehead and the jaw. This indicates anxiety and disbelief.

■ Smiling. This is a sign of relaxation and willingness to proceed.

■ Increased eye contact. This is a sign of interest, providing it is not staring or glaring.

Body language continued

5 CHANGES IN VOCAL TONE

Changes in tone are clear sign of approval or disapproval because the voice conveys a lot of emotion, which is very hard to mask. Look for these signals:

■ People speak confidently when discussing issues they are happy or satisfied with.

■ People lower their tone, along with their volume, when they are talking about difficult issues.

■ People speak with broken, faltering sentences when they are not confident in what they are saying.

■ People raise their voices, and their volume, when they are speaking passionately about an issue that is important to them. This is an important sign—do not mistake this for anger or aggression.

■ Anger is immediately obvious; it can be both loud (shouting) and quiet (dangerous lowering of tone).

EXERTING YOUR OWN INFLUENCE

1 **ADOPT THE RIGHT POSTURE**
This encourages your opponent to enter into rapport with you, which opens the channels of communication.

■ Maintain an open posture, with your hands in your lap.

■ Maintain an upright (but not stiff) body position, which shows you are alert to what your opponent is saying.

■ Maintain a calm demeanor, which means not making any sudden movements or gestures.

■ Avoid crossing your arms and legs as this symbolizes a barrier between you and your opponent.

■ Avoid slouching, which suggests a lack of interest.

■ Avoid resting your head on your hand, which shows you are not paying attention.

2 USE FACIAL EXPRESSIONS TO YOUR ADVANTAGE

Your own facial expressions are just as important as your ability to read your opponent's face.

■ Engage in eye contact, but don't stare or glare.

■ Relax your face, and maintain an open expression.

■ Don't be afraid to smile—it is infectious and will help create a relaxed atmosphere.

■ Hold your head in a steady position.

■ Gently nodding at certain moments can help encourage a reticent opponent to speak.

■ Don't react too strongly if you are told something shocking.

■ Avoid dropping your jaw or rolling your eyes if you hear something you disagree with.

PRACTICE MAKES PERFECT

It is best to sit and practice controlling your posture, tone, and facial expressions for a variety of situations. Sit in front of the mirror and examine what you look like every time you hear a different piece of news across the spectrum, from good to completely disastrous.

Everyone can smile and look relaxed when the news is good: "Yes, we can accommodate your wish to bring the delivery date forward," but think about how you are going to control yourself if you are being stonewalled or bullied, the meeting has become fractious, or something unexpected happens: "That is a completely unacceptable proposal. I have already told your boss we cannot operate on those terms. I demand to speak to him on the phone right away!"

You may not want to give away your true feelings, but by adopting a relaxed but alert posture, and not just reacting to what your opponent has said, you will exert influence over the meeting by helping it to be conducted in a positive way.

Applying the signals

So how do these signals translate into action? You have to know when to press home an advantage, when to back off, and when to do more work. You need to work toward a green light situation, where you have reached agreement on a key issue. These are the signals in a nutshell:

THESE ARE THE "INTERESTED— TELL ME MORE" SIGNALS:

■ Open postures with palms facing up

■ Forward, open body movement

■ Alert facial expressions

■ Upright posture

■ Moderate vocal tone

■ Engaged eye contact

THESE ARE THE "GREEN LIGHT— WE HAVE AGREEMENT" SIGNALS:

■ Sudden relaxation in facial expressions

■ Sudden relaxation in body posture

■ Sitting back in the chair with open posture

■ Changing a closed posture to an open one

■ Sudden relaxation in vocal tone accompanied by a reduction in the pace of speech

THESE ARE THE "RED LIGHT—WE HAVE NO AGREEMENT" SIGNALS:

- Relaxed smile

- Relaxed eye contact

- Gentle nodding of the head

- Lessening of tension in the shoulders

- Unclenching of fists

- Sudden end to fidgeting

- Relaxed sigh

- Closed postures with palms facing down

- Stiffening in body position

- Stiffening of facial features

- Sitting back in chair with closed posture

- Low vocal tone

- Fast speech

- Break in eye contact

Asking questions (II)

As we've seen, asking questions and listening is the key to unearthing your opponent's interests. This constant information-gathering enables you to work out her weaknesses and strengths as the meeting progresses.

OPEN-ENDED QUESTIONS

The best way to ask questions is to use "open-ended" questions. These questions encourage a detailed response. They are the opposite of "closed" questions, which only encourage a "Yes" or "No" answer. Open-ended questions often start with "Who," "What," "When," "How," and "Where."
These are some examples:

"How do you think we can work around this problem?"

"What do you regard as the most important issue here?"

"Where can we find common ground on this issue?"

All these questions encourage a response that is more than just a single word. As a word of caution, be careful about using "Why," because this can imply you are demanding an explanation, and it sounds like an accusation. Instead, say: "What are the reasons for . . . ?" or "How do you understand the situation regarding . . . ?"

Go back to the list of key issues you developed in Chapter 2 (see pp. 24–29 and pp. 88–91). For the sake of argument, imagine you are a buyer negotiating with a manufacturer who wishes to sell you a new product. These are the issues you may have listed:

1 Price

2 Quantity

3 Delivery or distribution

4 Payment terms

5 Competition

Asking questions (II) continued

THE IDEA IS TO USE OPEN QUESTIONS TO TEST THE BOUNDARIES OF YOUR
OPPONENT'S CLAIMS AND TO WORK OUT HOW IMPORTANT YOUR BUSINESS
IS TO YOUR OPPONENT IN EACH OF THESE FOUR KEY AREAS. FOR EXAMPLE:

1 PRICE
"What is your current pricing policy?"
"What is the structure for discounts?"
"If we were to double our order, what price would you quote?"

2 QUANTITY
"What percentage of your manufacturing output would an
order of 1,000 units represent?"
"If we were to repeat our order once a year for five years, what
would that do to unit cost?"

3 DELIVERY OR DISTRIBUTION
"Who handles your distribution?"
"What are your current delivery terms?"
"Where is your warehouse based?"
"What other companies do you deliver to?"

4 THE COMPANY AND ITS COMPETITION
"Who else supplies this kind of product?"
"How long have you been operating in this market?"
"What is your current market share?"
"What are your plans for cornering more market share?"

All these open questions, and the answers to them, will help you determine your position relative to your opponent's. You may find that she is stronger in some areas than in others. Look out for hesitation in her answers, which may indicate a weakness.

Getting your point across

So far, we have dealt with listening and acknowledging your opponent's point of view. Once you've heard her out, its time to get your views and opinions across. Again, this requires skill and patience. You have to make sure that your response keeps her eyes and ears open and does not make her defensive.

1 **LOOK AT HOW YOU THINK**
Typically, we tend to think that there are only two solutions to a negotiation: either my point of view or her point of view. This is called the either-or way of thinking, and you need to avoid it in your meeting—it boxes in your thinking. For example, if your opponent says:

"You can have either a lower price or a lower quantity, but you can't have both," you can reply:

"I can see your predicament. In my experience, I have seen a low price on a low quantity lead to a long-term relationship, which produces excellent benefits."

This maneuvers you away from the either-or mindset.

2 INCLUDING YOUR OPPONENT'S VIEW
If someone says something you don't like and you think you are being reasonable, and have practiced acknowledging techniques (see pp. 98–99 and 129), you may say something along the lines of:

"I appreciate that you do not want to offer low prices on low quantities, but I cannot afford to pay any more."

The word "but" is the problem here. All you have done is to contradict what your opponent has said, which closes her ears. Instead, agree with her position, and use the word "and." This has the effect of including your opponent's view into your own, which will help keep her listening.

Say:

"That's right, low prices on low quantities is what I am looking for and what this gets you is a long-term relationship."

3 TALK ABOUT YOURSELF, NOT YOUR OPPONENT

To make sure that your opponent's ears stay open, describe your thoughts and feelings, rather than attempt to describe hers. This means you use the word "I," not the word "you." So in our example, if your opponent says:

"I cannot offer you the low price you want if you order only a low quantity," avoid saying:

"You are not helping find a solution to this problem."

Instead say:

"The way I see the issue is that if we can agree on the low price and the low quantity, a long-term relationship will be the result," or:

"I feel that there are wider benefits to be considered than just price and quantity."

It is a question of not contradicting your opponent or putting her on the defensive, but of offering another perspective.

4 SAY WHERE YOUR DIFFERENCES LIE

When two people disagree in a delicate negotiation, the temptation is either to tip-toe around the issue without acknowledging it for fear of upsetting the other party or to lock horns in outright hostility. Neither is a successful negotiating ploy.

Instead, simply state where your areas of disagreement are. This does not have to be done aggressively, just as a matter of fact and clarity. If you do not know exactly where you disagree, how can you hope to find a resolution? Say something like:

"I understand that we haven't reach a deal on low price and low quantity. I understand your concerns, and I have also put my point of view across. I think we can reach an understanding though if we put our heads together."

This may just be the spur that the negotiation needs to find a solution.

in the meeting

The power game

Using persuasion is the key to effective negotiation, but what happens if this does not work? Typically, negotiators turn to powerplays—you cannot get anywhere by persuasion, so force, threat, and coercion become the order of the day.

TYPES OF POWER
Learning about the different types of power will help you learn about your own deficiencies. This list of five types of power was created by two sociologists, French and Raven, in 1959.

1 COERCIVE POWER
This is the power to force someone to do something against her will, either by taking action against her, or by withdrawing something from her. Gaining compliance is the key. In the business world, coercive power is used by senior management to get staff to do their jobs. In negotiation, it is wielded by a large company over a smaller one in order to get the smaller one to agree to a one-sided agreement.

2 REWARD POWER

Similar to coercive power, dependency is created by giving rewards—often economic—for good performance or behavior. The withdrawal of, or threat of withdrawing, such rewards, or the threat of, can be used coercively. Systems of reward are common in business, and also in negotiating. One company may "reward" another for doing business with it, but should this business be refused, the reward is withdrawn, with potentially damaging consequences.

3 LEGITIMATE POWER

Legitimate power is typically seen in people in positions of authority, from presidents to the police to CEOs of large companies. In business, it is assumed that these people have a right to exercise control, which may often spill over into the negotiating process and tip the balance in their favor.

The power game continued

4 REFERENT POWER

This is personal power and is created by charisma, fame, or the ability to generate admiration. Social leaders often have this power. In the business world, influential company executives often have referent power, making people listen to them and defer to them. This is a powerful "people" tool in a negotiating context, but be aware that charisma is not confined just to senior management.

5 EXPERT POWER

Expert power comes from having knowledge, information, or skill of value to someone else. This makes it a very valuable tool. It creates dependency: One side has the knowledge, the other side wants it. In business, it is seen in a range of situations from job interviews to R&D departments, as well as at the negotiating table. The side with the knowledge wields considerable power over the side that wants it.

6 OTHERS

There are other forms of power that are usually evident during negotiations. One side will seek to control the environment in which the negotiation is taking place by making the other side uncomfortable or unwelcome. One side may seek alliances with a third party and use this combined power as a negotiating weapon. Or the opponent may seek to control the meeting or the agenda by dictating proceedings.

All of these types of power are regularly used by negotiators in a wide range of business situations, from interviews to managing staff to closing deals with other companies.

Don't assume that if your opponent is from a large, rich company, and that if you are from a small, relatively poor one, that you have no power to influence the negotiation—we will look in more detail at how to exert this influence over the coming pages in this section.

It must be stressed that exerting influence does not guarantee success; it is just a way of ensuring that you maximize your chances of success.

The power game continued

POWER IS A PERCEPTION
The power people "have" is often a matter of assumption. This knowledge allows people who wish to wield power to create a perception of power. On the back of this, they deliberately cultivate the notion that they have power, without ever explicitly having to say why they are so important.

WE PERCEIVE PEOPLE TO BE IN A POSITION OF POWER WHEN:

1

THEY LOOK POWERFUL
This generally involves wearing expensive clothes, arriving in an expensive car (a chauffeur-driven one makes them look incredibly important), wearing an expensive watch, inviting you to an expensive restaurant or other important corporate entertainment. They may also have an entourage of aids or advisers, which enhances their appearance of power.

2 THEY ACT POWERFULLY

This involves projecting their personalities, positions, and the companies they work for as major players. The CEO of a large company will not wait to be asked to take a seat or to speak. She will assume authority over a negotiator whom she perceives has less power. Likewise, the negotiator who perceives her opponent to be less experienced will seek to exploit this.

REDRESS THE BALANCE

Start by wearing expensive clothes yourself, hiring an expensive car, or confidently ordering wine from the list at the expensive restaurant.

Consider this example. A small producer of organic fruit confronts a supermarket buyer playing power games. The producer confounds the buyer's expectations by turning up smartly suited and behaving professionally—not with dirty fingernails and driving a pick-up truck. In the buyer's eyes, she is now not just a farmer, but a successful businesswoman. The pendulum of power has already started to swing back toward the producer.

So how can the producer of organic fruit persuade the buyer that power is not an effective tool at the negotiation table?

The answer lies in making the buyer aware of the consequences of failure to reach agreement.

This may sound far-fetched. To the buyer, failure to reach agreement with a small producer might seem unimportant—it would have a negligible impact on the supermarket's bottom line. To the producer, passing up the opportunity to reach an agreement with a major client would seem foolish. Before the producer lets her arm be twisted, though, she can remind herself of several things:

1 The buyer is interested in making a deal. She would not be at the table if she wasn't. If the buyer says: "This is a waste of time. We will not pay that much per pound. Take or leave the offer," the producer can remind the buyer that what really is a waste of time is taking the time to conduct negotiation but needlessly leaving empty-handed, when both producer and buyer have a mutual interest in doing business.

2 The producer may be growing a luxury fruit—a niche market product— that the buyer knows will attract premium prices, so profits margins are still high. Because the market for luxury fruit may be growing, it is in the buyer's interests to reach a long-term agreement with the producer. So the producer asks the buyer:

"What would happen to your profits and future growth in this sector of the market if you walk away empty-handed?"

3 The buyer may have traveled a long way to the producer's farm. Does she want to face another long journey to another farm, where she also may not reach an agreement? The producer asks:

"Where will you go next if you walk away empty-handed?"

126
in the meeting
The power game continued

4

There may only be a handful of growers of this luxury fruit. If the buyer breaks off the negotiation, the producer again asks the buyer:

"Where will you get this product if you walk away empty-handed?"

5

The producer reveals her BATNA:

- She is aware that demand for this product is growing and has other interested parties—she can always sell to another supermarket.
- Her reputation locally is good and local demand for her fruit may be high, so her business is already turning a profit.
- She doesn't need to rush into a one-sided agreement with the supermarket—a very good position to be in.
- The producer asks the buyer: "What do you think I will do if I can't reach agreement with you?" She then explains the situation.

6 The producer warns the buyer that failure to reach agreement is not in the interests of either party, stating clearly the facts of the situation. This keeps the argument objective and focused on the situation, not on the people negotiating.

In effect, this stops the warning from sounding like a threat, which will only make the buyer defensive.

The buyer's powerplay is now not looking so effective. At this point, the producer has influenced the negotiation sufficiently to revert to the technique of persuading the buyer that doing business is a "win-win" situation.

Of course, the stronger the producer's position, the greater the chance she has of pulling this off. This is why preparation before the meeting and development of effective techniques such as a BATNA are so important.

Conversation techniques

Having seen what powerplays look like, and how you can find areas in which you have power as well, these are some conversation ideas for getting your opponent to come around to the idea that persuasion techniques are the way to do conduct the negotiation.

1   ESTABLISH THE FACTS BY INVITING DISCUSSION
    Remember, you are constantly trying to get your opponent over to your side. To do this, you must not provoke a defensive reaction. So don't just present the facts as you see them—make sure you get them right. This means checking by simply asking questions. By involving your opponent, you will start to win her over onto your side. Say:

    "Help me out here—am I right in thinking that we agreed $10 a unit?"

    "Correct me if I'm wrong, but I understood that $10 a unit was the price that we agreed?"

2

OFFER SOME PERSONAL APPRECIATION

Do this by acknowledging previous good business or some flexibility shown to your company when it needed it. Showing appreciation is a sign that the other side has earned your approval, which will win them over to your side, even though they may not, on the face of it, seem to need your approval. Say:

"We appreciate the way you were prepared to be flexible at the last minute over the delivery of the last consignment."

"I'd like to thank you for the consideration you showed over extending the delivery deadline."

3 STICK TO A PRINCIPLE

This is far more effective than quibbling over money, time, conditions, or any of the negotiable details of a deal. It also:

- Shows that any movement must be also on the basis of fair reasoning.
- Negates the use of power, which is often used by the more powerful side whenever it suits her.
- Confirms that you are not interested in doing business on the basis of self-interest, greed, or egotism—reassurance that you are seeking a "win-win" outcome.

Say:

"We want to be assured that a fair balance will be struck between the money we are paid and goods we provide."

"Nobody likes being cheated. Let's agree that we will conduct this negotiation on principles of fairness for a 'win-win' outcome."

4 KEEP ASKING QUESTIONS, KEEP SUMMING UP
Keep asking questions that will get to heart of the matter and
stop you from presenting facts and ideas as a *fait accompli*,
which will only put your opponent on the defensive. Each time
you get to a suitable point, sum up what you have discussed. Do
so without rancor and present only the facts as agreed. Say:

"What is the underlying thinking behind your opinion?"

"What are the interests we are trying to satisfy here?"

"Where are the principles we agreed on?"

"Let me see if I have got this straight—we have agreed $10 per
unit, but are undecided as to what comprises a unit?"

Conversation techniques continued

5 DON'T MAKE SNAP DECISIONS

Resist making snap decisions, even if you are being strong-armed. Quick decisions are usually regretted decisions, so create a bit of gap between the proposal and your answer. Don't, however, appear indecisive or lacking the authority to make a decision. This will weaken your standing. Instead, make a reasonable sounding excuse, and make it confidently. Say:

"You have presented me with figures that I need to run through my spreadsheet back at the office. Once my PA has done this, I will have an answer for you. Please excuse me while I make a call. I will have an answer for you in an hour."

6 PRESENT SOLUTIONS BASED ON PRINCIPLES AND FAIRNESS
When suggesting a solution or making a proposal, spell out the principles that you are using. This shows that you are motivated by reason, rather than self-interest. Also, make it clear that your solution is one possibility, rather than the definitive answer—this is not a game of who can appear to be the cleverest. Say:

"Given the reasoning we have used, can I suggest that one solution is that a palette of ten boxes constitutes a unit, for which we will pay $10."

"The idea I have in mind is to consider that $10 will buy me ten boxes, which we can consider to be one unit."

Conversation techniques continued

7 MAKE IT EASY FOR THEM TO SAY "YES"
Threats rarely produce a "yes" from your opponent. They put your opponent on the defensive and do not pave the way for an agreement. Try to make it easy for her to say "yes." Spell out what will happen if you reach agreement (you will both benefit) and what will happen if you don't (you will both lose out needlessly). Say:

"If we agree to $10 a unit, we can move on to looking at favorable delivery times."

"If we can't agree on $10 a unit, then we cannot offer any favorable delivery times."

8 LEAVE ON A GOOD NOTE
People always remember their first and last impressions of you. So leave the meeting or the discussion on the point in question on a good note, no matter how fractious the meeting has been. It makes the right impression, shows you have not been cowed by powerplays, and leaves the door open for the future. Say:

"Thank you very much for your time—our meetings have been very constructive."

"It's been great thrashing out all our interests, and I'm really pleased we can now see where agreement might lie. I hope it will open more doors in the future."

Continuing information gathering

We have seen how important gathering information is prior to the meeting, but it is very important that this continues during the meeting, right from the start to the end. It is particularly relevant when a negotiation is conducted across a series of meetings.

1 Information gathering needs to be a continuous process. Keep asking the questions outlined on pp. 38–39 and 110–113.

2 Be mindful of making assumptions—keep checking that you do not get lulled into a false sense of security by thinking that "I know where this conversation is headed." Many negotiators make great efforts to avoid making assumptions at the start of the meeting, but lose concentration by the end.

3 Make notes as you go along. Having accurate information in front of you will help you come to the right conclusions when you have time to review what was said in the meeting. If you feel confident or think that making an obvious note would be too conspicuous, commit what was just said to memory. To buy time before the conversation moves on, and to make sure you fully understand what was said, ask questions about the point.

4 Don't be afraid to ask for time-out at a suitable point if you feel that a vital piece of information has just come your way and you need a few minutes of quiet time to digest its meaning.

5 Consider what the impact of the information you have just learned will be on your game plan. Unexpected pieces of information may force you to change your approach, but be careful not to overreact and attempt to start from a clean slate.

Staying on track

Not getting knocked off track is one of the challenges you will face as a negotiator. All negotiations, no matter how well planned, will involve some tangental conversations. Recognizing them, dealing with them, and not being derailed by them requires considerable practice because some of these tactics may be deliberately introduced by your opponent to throw you off course.

1 DECIDE WHAT IS THE ESSENCE OF THE NEGOTIATION
Work out during the discussion what points are most relevant to the outcome you want to achieve. All the extraneous issues are the irrelevant parts of the conversation.

As your discussion progresses, ask yourself: "Is this issue really relevant to the agreement I am trying to reach?"
If it is not, then:

■ First acknowledge it.
■ Do not try to dismiss the aside out of hand and force the conversation back to the main topic. This is too obvious and will make your opponent defensive and inclined to want to discuss the aside at length.
■ Find a way back to the main point.

2 RECOGNIZE THE USE OF OFF-THE-POINT CONVERSATIONS
In addition to acknowledging asides, you can use them to your advantage. All negotiators are people, and unremittingly intense discussions may not necessarily produce the result you want. So remember:

- Light tangental conversations can be really useful—a quick story or anecdote will often lighten the mood during a tense period and can ease the main conversation along.
- However, remind yourself that this is only of limited value. Do not dwell on it, and quickly return to the main issue, using the break in tension as the impetus.

Staying on track continued

3 DON'T GET CARRIED AWAY

It is equally important not to veer off track. This can happen
when a negotiation is going too well, and you get carried away
with the momentum of it all. You may end up:

■ Giving away too many concessions
■ Not getting the best deal you can
■ Signing up for more than you had originally wanted

The classic example of this is the 3-for-2 offer in stores. You
might have only wanted to buy one T-shirt, but you are wowed
by the special offer. If you take up the offer, you end up with
three times as many T-shirts as you originally needed, and have
spent twice your original budget.

The same can happen during a negotiation, so:

■ Remind yourself of your original aims
■ Make sure that you yourself are not the person responsible
  for wandering from them

4

DON'T LET PERSONAL ISSUES GET IN THE WAY

Your primary concern is to conduct a successful negotiation, so don't let personal problems with your opponent get in the way. This can happen in two main ways:

■ You may feel that your opponent has tried to trick you or has insulted you in some way.
■ Perhaps there may be some previous history of antagonism between you. It is easy to get caught up in the desire to retaliate.

Both of these will inevitably take you off course and jeopardize finding a mutually beneficial agreement.

WHAT TO SAY

Staying on track requires considerable abilities in conversation management and is something you need to practice. Suppose you are in a situation where you are trying to negotiate the sale of computer equipment to a client you have supplied before. The conversation could run like this:

1

YOU:
"I think we have resolved our disagreement over the month for delivery of the equipment." (Trying to sum up the issue under discussion.)

OPPONENT:
"Yes, but we haven't discussed how many batches the whole delivery will comprise." (Introducing a side issue that may derail the discussion.)

2

YOU:
"You're right, we haven't talked about that yet, and that is something that we need to sort out." (Acknowledging that the point needs discussion, but at a later date.)

OPPONENT:
"I want the delivery in four batches, on May 4, May 14, May 21, and May 24." (Interrupting and attempting to force discussion of side issue.)

3

YOU:
"I will make a note of what you have requested. This is one of several specific details still to be sorted out as regards the contract. May I suggest that we deal with these at our next meeting?" (Attempting to put the discussion back on track by suggesting a date for discussing the side issue, and moving back to the main issues.)

OPPONENT:
"No, I would prefer to sort out exact dates now." (Flatly refusing all attempts to move back to the central issues.)

Staying on track continued

4 YOU:
"Okay, let's give this ten minutes, and then let's return to the agenda items we agreed on before the meeting." (Further acknowledging the opponent's concerns, conceding some time to discuss them, before reminding him gently of the agenda.)

OPPONENT:
"I'm not prepared to let this drop. During our last negotiation, you attempted to control the agenda with no regard for the wishes of my company." (Moving away completely from the negotiation and launching a personal attack on your integrity.)

5

YOU:

"My purpose is to clearly set out the issues to be discussed and save us both a lot of time and effort as a result. I believe that this is in both our interests, not just mine. I'm sorry that this is a bone of contention, but I feel that we have the potential to agree on so much that it seems a shame to fall out over a small point of procedure like this.

"I would therefore like to suggest that we move on to the next agenda item at the end of the ten minutes we have allotted for discussing the four delivery batches." (Keeping calm, not fighting back, pointing out the mutually beneficial nature of intentions, the wider issue of the agreement as a whole, before attempting again to get the conversation back on track.)

LEARNING YOUR LINES
Although you should never script what you are going to say in a negotiation (you have too much to lose if you fail to engage the other side), there are certain turns of phrase that you should practice to yourself. It is important to have them ready when you need them. These invariably:

1 Point out the mutual benefit of the item under discussion or a point of procedure.

"I believe that this is in both our interests, not just mine."

2 Stop you from reacting in a defensive, argumentative way.

"I agree that the point you have raised is an issue."

3 Allow you to keep calm, and therefore think clearly, while under pressure, or even under personal attack.

"I would like to suggest this as a working solution that I hope will suit us both."

4 Allow you to move the conversation along in a positive fashion, rather than to succumb to the negative tactics of your opponent.

"May I suggest that we take a little time to address your concerns, then return to our original discussion."

Framing and conceptualization

How well you can persuade your opponent depends on the key negotiating skill of framing. Framing is a method of presenting information in a way that is most likely to ensure that it is received favorably.

The classic example of the power of framing is the Coca-Cola that is twice as expensive in the fashionable downtown bar as it is in the neighborhood pub. The drink is the same in both places, but the surroundings—the "frame"—are different enough for us to think that it is worth paying double what we know we could get the goods for elsewhere.

Remember that negotiation is a process, not an outcome, and that framing allows you to alter the path the process is taking. Framing is an important tool and, practiced and used well, is often the difference between effective and ineffective negotiating.

THESE ARE THE RULES:

1

DON'T DISAGREE WITH YOUR OPPONENT'S POSITION
Because disagreeing leads to defensiveness, acknowledge your
opponent's position is a reasonable one and take it seriously.
Many negotiators will be taken by surprise that you have not
just simply dismissed their position and insisted on your own.

2

TURN YOUR OPPONENT'S POSITION INTO A PROBLEM-SOLVING IDEA
Instead of confronting your opponent's position by meeting it
head on with your own, try to view her position as an
opportunity to brainstorm the problem. Thus both parties
attempt to find a solution together, rather than just attempt to
impose solutions on one another.

Alternatively, you can ask your opponent for her advice. This
acknowledges her expertise and invites her to come up with
solutions to problems created by her position. Say:

"You are the expert on the production side. How would you go
about solving quality problems?"

3 USE QUESTIONS TO GET TO THE BOTTOM OF THE PROBLEM
So how do you get the discussion going and avoid the usual pattern of defensiveness? Ask these types of questions to get to the heart of the matter:

"What leads you to . . . ?" (What leads you to say that?)

"Can you help me . . . ?" (Can you help me understand your reasoning?)

"What if . . . ?" (What if we increased quality and decreased quantity?)

"What is . . . ?" (What is your thinking behind this?)

"How can we . . . ?" (How can we solve this problem together?)

"What can we . . . ?" (What can we do to get around this problem?)

4

USE IMAGES, METAPHORS, OR SHORT STORIES TO ILLUSTRATE YOUR POINT
Framing and reframing works best when accompanied by an
illustrative story or metaphor. Favorites are based on:

–Trees with branches that can bend in a storm (to demonstrate
strength through flexibility).

–The roots of a tree (to demonstrate the depth of a relationship
and/or hidden strength).

–Houses made out of bricks rather than sticks (to demonstrate the
worth of quality and longevity, even if they carry a higher price).

–Day, night, sunrise, and twilight (to demonstrate timelines and
to frame where you are in the negotiation).

You can of course make up your own. Skillful negotiators
research their opponent's negotiating style, personality, and
interests and use suitable framing metaphors. If, for example,
your opponent is a hard negotiator and a sports fan, use
metaphors that revolve around results-based action on the
sports field.

Knowing when to be objective

In any kind of principled, persuasive negotiation, much of what you say and claim will be based on reason rather than on ego or defensive positioning. Underpinning reason is objective, measurable criteria—the kind of evidence a lawyer might rely on.

OBJECTIVE, MEASURABLE CRITERIA IS:

■ Based on fact

■ Independent of the positions of either party

It is very difficult for your opponent to stick to a position if you can show that the facts she is basing her argument on are incorrect.

THESE ARE SOURCES OF OBJECTIVE CRITERIA:

■ Research (but not your own)

■ Expert opinion

■ Professional standards

■ Trade association guidelines or standards

■ Previous experience

■ The relevant law

■ Recognized data

■ Comparable situations

Try also to make sure that your evidence is practically applicable. This means that it must:

- Be comprehensible to both sides

- Lead to a real-world solution

- Lead to equal treatment of both sides

USING OBJECTIVITY

Although objectivity and the evidence it produces is important, be careful not to try to blind your opponent with science. Remember that you are trying to reach a mutually beneficial agreement, not present the evidence as if you were in a court of law. Doing so will only antagonize your opponent.

Knowing when to be objective continued

TO AVOID THIS OUTCOME, SKILLFUL NEGOTIATORS RECOMMEND THAT YOU:

1 Only produce your strongest material. Any weaker material will look suspect and make your opponent think that the strong material is therefore questionable, too.

2 Keep it brief. Long discourses on the credibility of your evidence will only irritate your opponent.

3 Introduce your material at the right point. Simply providing your opponent will reams of documentation be self-defeating if it is introduced at the wrong moment. This will quickly undermine your credibility. Remember that you are a negotiator, not a prosecutor.

4 Appreciate that your own evidence may not be the only material available on the issue. Your opponent will no doubt have her own evidence to back up her own interests.

5 Use your material as a starting point for finding the right agreement and influencing the process rather than as a tool for entrenching your own position.

This last point is very important. You may have to agree on which standards are the most suitable for your particular scenario and stick to them. By agreeing to use a set of standards as the basis for finding an agreement, you are circumventing the fixed-position scenario, which uses no such standards. In short, you are creating a common set of objective criteria that establishes the rules of the game, which you can refer back to if the negotiation starts to stall or wander off track.

Knowing the value of subjectivity

Objectivity alone will not always win the day: The element of subjectivity in any negotiation is often underestimated, even by negotiators who have all the facts at their fingertips.

EXAMPLES OF THE POWER OF SUBJECTIVITY IN NEGOTIATING:

1 The woman who has built her own company from scratch is unlikely to be tempted to sell her business on the basis of cash alone. Her emotional input into building her "baby" is such that she is more likely sell to a buyer who will give it the same care and attention.

2 Members of a trade union are less likely to want to deal sympathetically with company management that has treated them unfairly (perhaps sacked some of them) during a labor dispute, even if the union receives positive assurances that no further unfair treatment will take place.

3   An interviewee whose resumé looks superb on paper is less likely to get a job offer if she shows little or no enthusiasm for the job during the interview. Employers look for enthusiastic, committed people as well as people with the right skills and experience.

Clearly, the woman who has built her own business will not reject a cash offer if it is a very generous one; the business partnership may still be renewable if the contract is sound; and the trade union members can be won over given the right assurances from management. The point is that people representing their companies are passionate about their jobs, products, and services. Skillful negotiators will tap into this vein and marry subjectivity to objectivity to make a successful outcome more likely.

Can I trust you?

Trust plays an important part in all negotiations, but it does not mean that you should take what your opponent tells you, unquestioningly, at face value. It means that you can establish a credible working relationship with your opponent, and believe that she is acting with verifiable honesty and integrity.

THESE ARE SIGNS OF A TRUSTWORTHY OPPONENT:

1

A GOOD REPUTATION
Check to see how your opponent has behaved in previous negotiations either with your company or with another one.

2

RELIABILITY
Check to see if promises are kept and contractual terms honored.

3

SINCERITY
Check to see if your opponent is walking the walk, not just talking the talk. Again, doing what you say you are going to do engenders trust.

4

BREACHES OF TRUST
Check to see if your opponent has tried to change the game or manipulate you by reneging on an agreement, especially if it was timed to hit you at a weak moment.

5 HONEST COMMUNICATION
In addition to not telling blatant lies, check to see if your opponent is really attempting to make herself understood. Any deliberate ambiguity on her part means trust may be hard to build.

6 BEHAVIOR
Is your opponent behaving in a way that is moving the negotiation forward? These behaviors include the way in which she is speaking (clearly and with respect), how she is listening (is your point of view being heard?), and any nonverbal signs (her body language and facial expressions).

7 NONEXCESSIVE CONTROL
Check to see if your opponent is trying to exert too much control over the negotiation. Constant attempts to rearrange meeting times and places and to introduce new demands should be viewed with suspicion.

8 RESPECT FOR YOUR VIEW
If your opponent can see and acknowledge your point of view, even if she feels very strongly that her own is correct, she is showing that she is prepared to listen and understand.

Saving face

Saving face is the term commonly used to describe a reluctance to back down through fear of embarrassment, or loss of pride or status. It is another part of the anatomy of the human aspect of negotiating.

NO MATTER HOW EMBARRASSING YOUR GAFFE, SAVE FACE BY:

1

APOLOGIZING IMMEDIATELY
Acknowledge that you have made an error. Doing this straightaway will start the process of reconciliation as soon as possible. Expressly say that you got your facts wrong; make no comment on any other issue. Also, do not attempt to justify your error—you will only dig yourself in deeper by making it look as though the misunderstanding was caused by your opponent being misleading or unclear. Say:

"I apologize for my reaction to your proposal. I completely misinterpreted what you said."

2 CLARIFYING THAT YOU HAVE NOW GOT IT RIGHT
Having apologized, make sure you do not make the same
mistake again. Clarify that you have now understood what was
said by asking simple questions. You cannot continue until you
have the facts straight. Say:

"Let me make sure I am hearing you correctly this time, and
please correct me again if I am still off the mark. You have
said that . . . ."

3 THANKING THEM
Once you have got your facts straight, and very often you will
be put right by your bemused opponent without having to ask,
thank them for their input in explaining the situation to you.
Again, this closes the gap between you by acknowledging that
her explanation was of value to you. Say:

"Thank you for putting me right. I fully appreciate the
significance of the figures you have quoted."

4 USING THE NEW INFORMATION
Incorporate the information your opponent has just given you into a revised opinion or offer. This again closes the gap between you by showing that you have used what you have been told. Say:

"So, based on the figures you have just quoted, I would suggest that a figure of $10 per unit would suit us both."

5 GETTING BACK TO THE MATTER AT HAND
You do not need to dwell on your mistake. Promptly get back on track with the discussion, and put your mistake behind you. You have done all that you need to. Say:

"So, the next item on the agenda is delivery dates. We would like to suggest the following . . ."

Some negotiators are afraid to admit their mistakes for fear of appearing weak or stupid, or because they think it gives their opponent the upper hand. In fact, the opposite is true. You will earn respect from your opponent, which will actually allow you to influence the negotiation. In addition, you will be seen as a principled negotiator who is prepared to apply her rules to all situations, even when it seems that she is the loser.

As we have noted several times, the emotional aspects of a negotiation are very important. Engendering trust and respect, even at the risk of making yourself look a little foolish, will stand you in good stead for your future relationships with your opponent.

Further, in cross-cultural negotiations, cultivating respect may be an important component in gaining agreement, so do not be afraid to show respect.

Saving face continued

SAVING YOUR OPPONENT'S FACE

The second part of saving face is knowing how to save your opponent's face. Although this may not seem like your problem, skillful negotiators recognize that to get another person to alter her position they have to create a situation in which their opponent can back out without feeling humiliated. If this situation is not created, your opponent will not want to change her mind. Fear of what others will say if she does is her overriding concern. We all have to please others, so bear in mind the pressure not to give in that your opponent is facing. These are the kinds of people we are afraid of upsetting:

1 Your boss: "This deal isn't good enough. Why did you give in to those demands? I would never have done so. That's your promotion shelved!"

2 The members of the organization you represent: "You told us you could get us a 10 percent pay rise. Instead you've come back with a 5 percent one with lots of strings attached. You've sold us out! We'll never support you again!"

3 Family: "You've agreed to pay how much for that house? Why did you not involve me in the negotiation? This means I have to take on extra part-time work just to pay the mortgage!"

4 Own pride: "Why should I back down? She isn't backing down. I don't care how reasonable or clever her tactics are."

5 Friends: "I don't want to have to admit to another embarrassing failure—I had to admit to one last week!"

THESE ARE SOME TACTICS TO HELP YOU SAVE YOUR OPPONENT'S FACE:

1

SHIFTING SANDS
Suggest that your opponent is technically correct, but that changes to the situation are not of your making but beyond your control. This allows your opponent to blame any change of mind on the new circumstances, which could include:

- New laws
- Changing market conditions
- Changes to professional regulations
- Significant advances in production techniques

2

INDEPENDENT ADJUDICATOR
Appoint, or refer to, some kind of independent standard as a way of letting your opponent back down, knowing that an independent body has effectively made the decision for her. This is particularly useful when evaluating property, equipment, or building materials.

In financial circles, accountants and auditors exist specifically to do this. In smaller cases, market values are verifiable through trade magazines or newspapers.

3 SUGGEST SUITABLE EXPLANATIONS
Your opponent's fears about her colleagues' opinions may stop her from backing down. To a large extent, you can second-guess this criticism and offer suggestions to counteract it. Bear in mind these are only suggestions—do not put words in your opponent's mouth, or she will assume that you are manipulating her. By suggesting counterarguments, you can plant a seed that she can develop and take credit for.

4 REFRAME THE SITUATION
In a dispute over firefighters' pay, the union leader's demand for a substantial one-shot pay increase was denied. However, by offering a smaller pay raise up-front (back-dated for nine months) followed by a guaranteed future pay raise linked to changes in working practice, an agreement was reached; it allowed the union leader to present defeat of his original demand as overall long-term success for his members.

in the meeting

Buying time

All negotiators will at some time face a situation where they will feel that the process is moving too quickly or is showing signs of moving in the wrong direction. To counter this effect, you need to quickly buy yourself some time.

TRY THESE DELAYING TACTICS:

1 REPEAT WHAT HAS BEEN SAID
We have touched on this as a tactic for avoiding making wrong assumptions, but it also works very well for slowing the discussion down. Say:

"Can I just be clear on what is being said here. You are saying that .... Is that correct?"

This has the effect of creating a need for an answer from your opponent, which buys you even more time.

2   SPOT THE TRICK
It may well be the case that the discussion has sped up because
your opponent is trying to quickly introduce a controversial
subject that has not been previously discussed. Last-minute
demands and a glut of information are all ways opponents
"drop in" items into the discussion, hidden among other
information. Say:

"I don't believe that we have discussed the issue of reinsuring
the delivery—have I got that right?" or:

"I'm sorry, there are so many points here; can I just take you
back to where you said that insurance is not included in
your quote?"

Going back over the conversation and politely asking for
clarification quickly negates your opponents tricks.

Buying time continued

3

APPEAR TO MISUNDERSTAND
You can slow things down by appearing not to have fully understood what has been said or by claiming that you did not fully appreciate the implications of an earlier point. Say:

"I apologize—can I ask that we go over that point again?" or:

"There is a lot of information to take in here. Can I suggest that I take some notes so there is no further misunderstanding?"

4

CALL A HALT
This does not mean abruptly shouting "Stop!"; it is more a request for a time-out. Tack a little bit of flattery onto the front of your request to make it a bit more palatable to your opponent, who may not be wanting take a break at all. Say:

"That's a really good point, but I need extra figures sent over from the office before I can agree to it. Can we call a break for five minutes and I'll get an answer for you?" Or simply:

"I suggest a five minute break—I'd love another one of your excellent danishes and coffee."

5 DON'T RUSH

Even when you have bought some time, you still may not be in a position to make a decision. Having gone over all the salient points again, your opponent may well now try to rush you into a quick decision. After all, you're in full possession of the facts now, right?

Being rushed is a classic negotiation ploy and one you should resist at all costs, even if you feel that you cannot justifiably prevaricate any longer. Make every attempt to get out of the room, which has the natural effect of slowing the pace. Say:

"I need to run these figures past my accountant. Our company policy is to check figures first with the finance department," or:

"We usually ask for offers to be put in writing. To keep things moving, I'll just ring head office and get a decision for you."

172

Using gut feeling

Despite all your best preparation, the use of objective and subjective criteria, convincing figures, argument, and logic from both sides, there will always be times when something inside your mind is telling you that something is wrong.

So do you listen to this inner voice? Or just dismiss it as natural reticence as the time to seal the deal comes around? The answer is to listen to it. If you think that something is wrong, or conversely, if something appears to be going too smoothly, do not be afraid to question it. Questioning is the key to successfully interpreting gut instinct. Ask:

1 Why was such a fuss made of that simple point?

2 What was the body language like on that controversial point?

3 What was the response to my suggestion on that point?

4 Was her response in keeping with her general demeanor so far?

5 Why did she look agitated as she answered my question?

6 What was the level of eye contact on that crucial response?

7 What was her tone of voice as she put forward her suggestion?

In the first instance, if you think something is wrong and you can't put your finger on it, you need to buy yourself some time, using the tactics in the previous section.

Perhaps take a piece of paper and write down why you think things are not right or why you feel reticent about proceeding, and then let your mind do the talking.

in the meeting

Using humor

All negotiations become tense at some point. There is always a controversial issue that somehow cannot be resolved, and the temperature starts to rise. Some good humor can help break the tension.

THESE ARE THE BASIC FORMS OF HUMOR THAT WE ALL USE:

1 The quick quip. This is always something that rolls off the tongue on the spur of the moment, so it is difficult to prepare in advance.

2 The anecdote. This is a story that illustrates the point you are trying to make. Skilled negotiators will have a hat full of anecdotes ready for a variety of situations. Just make sure that you don't keep using the same tired stories everyone's heard before.

3 Irony. This is gently making a point by saying the opposite of what is actually the case. Juxtaposing two situations to make a humorous point has much the same effect.

4 Self-deprecation. This is making a joke at your own expense (though of course you don't have to make yourself look stupid) and is very useful if you feel you have been the one making all the clever points—it helps restore the balance and draws your opponent back into the discussion.

5 Bitter experience. You can create some light-hearted jokes by gently making fun of some bad (but not too bad) experience that you have had. This also marks you out as someone who is not too self-important.

Using humor continued

The flip side of the coin is that humor must be used wisely. It is easy to cause offense, particularly with people you hardly know and who are going to hold it against you if you slip up. So err on the side of caution, and keep your humor general and nonpersonal.

THESE ARE TYPES OF HUMOR YOU MUST AVOID USING:

1 Any quip or story that casts doubt on the parties around the table, their roles, the company they work for, or colleagues.

2 Comments that are designed to make you look clever—these automatically make everyone else feel beneath you.

3 Any comment at all that may be misconstrued as discriminatory. Subjects like politics, religion, gender, or age are not topics for jokes.

4 Any bad language, even if you think the other side can "handle it," or you have heard them swearing.

5 Anything that makes you look incompetent. You need to know where the line is between making gentle fun of yourself or a situation and embarrassing yourself.

6 Anything that shows you have behaved unethically. Jokes about how you pulled the wool over a previous opponent's eyes or how you pulled off some scam are out.

Dealing with conflict

Negotiations can become heated and strained, and those involved may become agitated and upset for a variety of reasons. Being able to handle heightened emotions and to spot potential areas of conflict before the meeting starts is a key skill.

Many negotiations take place against a backdrop of conflict and dispute; diplomatic talks try to end wars, and union leaders meet with management to try to end a strike. This makes applying the persuasion techniques of principled negotiation difficult. In practical terms, two angry opponents will not appear interested in searching for a mutually beneficial agreement.

However, skillful negotiators recognize that emotions are an inevitable part of all human interaction, not least during contentious negotiations, and know how to deal with them, even turning them to their own advantage.

These are some useful tips that will maximize your chances of a successful agreement in the face of conflict.

1

DON'T REACT
This is the golden rule. If you come under attack, simply retaliating will do nothing but inflame the situation, which will take you further away from a negotiated agreement, not closer. As we have seen, principled negotiation attempts to meet the interests behind positions; countering your opponent's position with one of your own will lead to a breakdown in talks.

2

RECOGNIZE HOW BOTH SIDES ARE FEELING
You (or your opponent) may be feeling upset for a number of reasons: broken promises, bad blood, or negative outside influences. This may be irritating you, making you want to lash out in anger, which in turn will only fuel your opponent's ire.

Recognize how you are feeling. Take a moment to note the issues that are upsetting you (before the meeting if necessary). Then, try to put yourself in your opponent's shoes. What are the pressures your opponent is facing? Note the likely sources of their grievances.

Dealing with conflict continued

3 EXPLAIN WHERE YOUR GRIEVANCES LIE
Say out loud where the sources of your anger or
disappointment lie, and invite them to do the same. Say:

"We believe your company reneged on the deal we had and are
angered by that. Can you help us understand where your anger
is coming from?"

An open discussion of sources of conflict is better than a highly
charged atmosphere where anger erupts at an inappropriate
moment that bears no relation to the source of grievance.
However, try to be sensitive to the best time to open this
conversation—it could be seen as provocative if you simply
start the meeting with a list of problems. This typically results
in retaliatory behavior from your opponent, who defensively
states his list of grievances in order to defend his position.

4 REFRAME THE ANGER

Be careful not to fall into the trap of thinking that because your opponent is angry about one issue that she feels the same way about all the issues in front of you. There is every chance that she may be well-satisfied with how other aspects of your negotiation are progressing. So it is important to realize this, and reframing the situation is useful here. Say:

"I know we disagree strongly on this point, but I don't believe it undermines the solid nature of our relationship," or:

"I'm glad we've got this out in the open. It highlights how honest our relationship has become," or:

"This is such a hot topic. I fully understand why you feel so strongly. I do too. We can sort this out in both our interests, just as we have done on all the other issues."

How to close the deal

After so much advice on creating a successful negotiating conditions, there remains the question of how to close the deal.

Having created the right conditions that enable your opponent to say "yes" to your proposals or created a set of proposals that are mutually beneficial, you still have to get her to sign on the dotted line.

This should, in some ways, be a simple process—there is nothing in theory to stop her from doing so, seeing as you will have already reached agreement on all the issues under discussion. However, bear in mind that this final obstacle may also be the most troublesome. Anyone can agree verbally to your suggestions. Putting pen to paper to make a firm commitment may be another issue.

THE ANSWER LIES IN:

1 KEEPING THE DESIRED END IN SIGHT
Think about what it is you are actually trying to achieve. Never take your eyes off the prize, but as we have said all along, your job as you go along is to build the ladder that will enable both you and your opponent to reach the top. The more mutually beneficial the steps and the process, the less problematic signing off on the final agreement will be.

2 USING DRAFT AGREEMENTS
If signing an agreement is too much of a step for your opponent, create a draft agreement. Make it crystal clear that it is only a draft, and that there is no obligation on the part of either side to agree to any of its clauses, all of which can be altered before there is any mention of signing. Keep refining the draft until both of you are happy. This will keep the clauses of the draft very much out in the open, making signing off on the final version less of a step for your opponent.

How to close the deal continued

3 NOT RUSHING

Allow your opponent some time to think about the implications of what she is agreeing to. If you attempt to pressure her, she is likely to get cold feet. It is generally better to move negotiations along at their natural pace than to force the issue. This will allow your opponent to:

- Think that she has had time to consider everything properly and discuss it with her boss or head office, making signing less of a big step.
- Recognize that the deal being struck is the best one available and doesn't ignore criteria that will become important later.

4 BEING FLEXIBLE

Setting out a strict timetable by which various parts of the negotiation have to be completed may be fine in terms of keeping tabs on where you have got to, but it is likely to put your opponent off. Exercising some flexibility will ease the pressure slightly on your opponent. A more relaxed opponent is more likely to sign on the dotted line.

5

ADDING A SWEETENER

This does not mean that you should offer gold Rolexes or first-class trips to the Caribbean. But be prepared to offer something on top of what you have already agreed as a way of overcoming any final hurdles. So, keep something in reserve, making sure it is in keeping with the basic logic of your discussion.

For example, in a negotiation on delivery dates of farm produce, promise your client exclusive use of your new fleet of high-tech refridgerated trucks to keep the goods in the best possible condition.

4

when things go awry

The nature of problems

Most of us do not like it when a situation is going wrong, or when we find we are the victims of a dirty trick. We often find it all the harder to deal with in a business situation when we sense that handling the situation badly may jeopardize the whole deal.

TYPICALLY THIS IS OUR REACTION TO PROBLEMS AND TRICKS:

1 Because we don't like them, we attempt to avoid them at any cost, even when they need to be dealt with.

2 We are upset by them when they occur, so we often attempt to side-step them rather than solve them.

3 We are often surprised when they occur, despite considerable experience of them in almost all other areas of our lives.

4 In the case of a negotiation, we attempt to avoid difficult problems by appeasing our opponent, and we end up giving away too much.

Dealing with problems and tricks requires these reactions to be put to one side. When you find you are faced with a situation that is going wrong:

1 Take a step back. Realize that a simple clash of interests may be the root cause of the problem.

2 Do not ignore or be upset by the emotional aspects inherent in any negotiation. Problems are likely to lead to displays of emotion.

3 Recognize that problems may arise. This will help you prepare for them and will stop you from being embarrassed or frightened by them if they do occur.

4 Recognize that problems may arise. This will help you stop reacting to them in a damaging way, either by retaliating or giving in.

5 Recognize that problems may occur. This will help you realize that resolving them is time you need to factor into the negotiation. This is always time well spent.

Dealing with deception

Deception is a word with a wide range of meanings. In the business context, it is the deliberate withholding or serious misrepresentation of key information, which, if we had it, would lead us to make a completely different decision.

Less clear is the dividing line between presenting information in a way that produces a competitive advantage and outright deception.

Deception is clearly designed to secure an agreement under false pretenses, which raises all sorts of legal issues for the future. Knowing that you are being deceived is upsetting. All attempts at establishing trust come to nothing, and this is a very difficult obstacle to overcome.

Of course, the ultimate sanction is to break off negotiations altogether. It is very difficult to find agreement with someone who proves to be persistently untrustworthy.

COMMONLY, THERE ARE TWO AREAS THAT CHARACTERIZE DECEPTION:

1

INCORRECT FACTS

Problem: You are at the negotiating table, and your opponent is busy feeding you figures that aren't true. He may say: "We can't possibly sell at $10 per unit" when you know that he is selling to a competitor at exactly that price.

Solution: Make the effort to check. If you can't check right away, say that you'll verify the figures at your first opportunity. Do not be afraid to do this—rest assured that your opponent will be doing the same. You do not have to conduct the negotiation in a spirit of mutual distrust, but be wary of taking statements at face value.

What to say: Never accuse your opponent of outright lies or of dishonesty. This challenges and insults him, and makes him defend his position or risk losing face. So instead, say:

"I have different information that I know I can rely on. Surely we can find a way around this sticking point?"

This shows that you are well-equipped with the real facts at hand and are willing to overlook your opponent's attempted deception in order to progress the negotiation.

Dealing with deception continued

2 LACK OF AUTHORITY
Problem: Just when you think you have reached full agreement, your opponent informs you that he's just off to phone the head office to get approval on all the concessions he has made. This is a ploy that allows your opponent a second chance at obtaining further concessions. "Head office" will, unsurprisingly, come back with a whole raft of changes to previously agreed issues.

Solution: Do not feel pressured into making any further concessions off the bat. This is a psychological ploy to grind you down—your disappointment in finding out that there is still more work to be done will make you vulnerable to making further concessions so that talks don't break down and the process hasn't been a waste of time. So do your homework before the meeting to find out how much authority your opponent really has.

What to say: Politely ask: "Can I just check that you have the authority to agree to the points raised here today?"

If the answer is "no", then simply ask to deal with someone who has the right authority or, at the very least, make clear that the meeting is a preliminary one to test the waters.

If you do not check and have this ploy sprung on you unexpectedly, say: "Notify me of any changes you would like to make. I will, of course, be doing the same."

Or even call into question the ethics of such a ploy. Say: "Would you consider your tactic acceptable if I used it on you?" However, this may be construed as adversarial, so make sure that you have explored other options first before saying this.

when things go awry

Bluffing

Bluffing is similar in nature to deception, but your opponent is simply trying to create a smokescreen, a false belief that his position is stronger than it really is, which he is daring you to challenge.

Bluffing can be very difficult to spot if done well, and those experienced at doing it, like good poker players, will know when to do it, and when to play it straight.

The flip side of this is that not many negotiators are that good at bluffing, so take heart that it is usually relatively easy to see through this trick.

1 EXAGGERATING

This is the standard bluff. Just as in poker, your opponent simply exaggerates what he holds in his hand in terms of cost, price, manufacturing time, delivery dates, and so on in the hope of forcing you into agreeing to a deal that suits him better.
It is very easy (and tempting) to bluff like this, but it is very difficult to make it stick. If your bluff is being called, it is very difficult to back down without losing face.

2 BLINDING YOU WITH SCIENCE

This involves hiding the real facts among a whole host of other unimportant facts and figures, such as prices, quantities, delivery dates, margins, percentages, production, third parties, and global distribution. The list is almost endless, and your opponent will attempt to exploit this by making up a few of his own, allowing him plenty of opportunity to bury the real story.

3 HURRYING YOU ALONG

Your opponent will not want to dwell too long on his bluff. In addition to mixing up the facts among a whole load of clutter, he will want to push the conversation along quickly as well. Having rattled through a variety of facts and figures, he may well concoct some spurious reason for needing a quick decision.

4 DISTORTING EMPHASIS

Some material may be presented as being much more important than others. This is often the case with graphs, bar charts, pie charts, and histograms, whose axes can be adjusted to make figures look greater or smaller than they actually are.

Bluffing continued

TO ROOT OUT BLUFFS:

1 ASK QUESTIONS
Don't go charging in and call your opponent a liar—this isn't a poker game in a Western movie. Keep calm and keep asking questions on points that seem suspect. Remember that if you come across something you don't understand, you have every right to keep questioning it until you do understand.

Constant questioning is one of the most effective techniques for uncovering the real facts. Say:

"Let me make sure I have the figures right. You are saying . . . ."

Or:

"I still don't understand where your concerns about profit margins come from. Can you please explain further?"

2 RECAP AND PAUSE—AS OFTEN AS YOU NEED TO

When you've got your answers, make sure that you are interpreting them correctly. It is very embarrassing to suspect that your opponent is bluffing, only to discover you have misused the evidence to support you own misconceptions.

So summarize what has just been discussed and confirm that your interpretation is correct.

You will also probably need some time to think about what you have just been told. Do not be afraid to give yourself some breathing space. Say:

"So correct me if I'm wrong, but the figures you have given me mean this ... (Pause.) Your profit margin is down by 25 percent. (Pause.) And the implication of this for me is that ...."

Bluffing continued

3 CHECK BODY LANGUAGE
Questioning, recapping, pausing, slowing down the pace, and creating a silence, as well as using effective information-gathering and assimilation techniques all have the effect of making your opponent sweat.

Bluffing is a high-risk strategy that your opponent would like to get over and done with as quickly as possible to avoid detection. Look for signs of agitation in his body language, such as:

■ Shifting around in his seat.
■ Being unable to make eye contact.
■ A rise in his tone of voice.
■ Sudden impatience to move on.

Very few people who try bluffing are actually any good at it—most do not have the ability to maintain a poker face for long.

4 MAKE SURE YOU HAVE PREPARED PROPERLY

If your research is thorough, you can quickly spot holes in your opponent's stories—you will know that it takes two months, not three, to manufacture your goods; that the cost per item is closer to $5 than it is to $10 and so on.

Once you have seen through the trick, your opponent invariably looks foolish. It is tempting to gloat at your success, but it is important not to humiliate him—this will make your opponent defensive, so do not press home your advantage in this way. It is enough that both of you realize what is going on. Say something like: "OK, so now we have more realistic figures, let's have a look at the other proposals you have made." It is very unlikely that your opponent will attempt another bluff. If your opponent does attempt to continue to try and bluff, it is a good idea to suggest taking a break. This will allow you time to consider how to deal with it. You should consider:

■ Drawing up a list of rules for the negotiation.
■ Gaining your opponent's agreement to abide by them.
■ If all else fails, consider breaking off the negotiation.

Dealing with last-minute changes

As with lack of authority, last-minute changes are deliberately designed to pressure you into thinking that to save the day you have to agree to a number of unexpected demands. Don't give in immediately.

Most negotiators will have come across this dirty trick at some point. You are happily concluding your deal, looking forward to celebrating back at the office, when, out of the blue, your opponent tells you that there has been a change of heart on some significant part of the negotiation. The excuses come in all sorts of guises, but these are some of the most common:

1 He has just found a supplier who can deliver exactly the same type of goods as you, to the same specification, but 10 percent cheaper.

2 He now needs a better specification for the goods he is buying but has no extra money to spend to cover the increased costs.

3 His company's profits are down and he has been informed that he has to place a smaller order but still wants the discount.

THERE ARE THREE POSSIBLE EXPLANATIONS:

1 Your opponent is simply trying to see if he can squeeze a little more out of you before putting pen to paper. If he succeeds, he'll have got a better deal at your expense; if he fails, he'll still have the original deal that he's happy with.

2 He's actually telling the truth. You must be very careful here. No opponent will tolerate your trying to call his bluff, no matter how politely, if he is expecting to be taken seriously. By not taking him seriously, you run the risk that the deal will collapse.

3 His last-minute demand is about what he really wants. He has been going along with your suggestions to make it look as though the process is going to be a success. This ploy plays on the fear that everything so far agreed might now be wasted.

Dealing with last-minute changes contir

THIS IS A DIFFICULT SITUATION TO DEAL WITH. SO HOW SHOULD YOU HANDLE I'

1 CALL A HALT

Don't react and certainly don't imply that he's just bluffing. It would be extremely embarrassing to do so only to find out that you are wrong. Instead, suggest that you call a halt to proceedings for a day or so while you have time to think about the new proposal. This will buy you time to:

■ Research his claims

■ Check to see if there really is any new competition

■ See what his company is really up to

In many cases, your preparation before the meeting should point you in the right direction. You will know whether there is any competition and will have obtained his company's literature, which will spell out its financial position and when it publishes its results.

2 ASSESS THE FALLOUT
Decide whether you can accommodate your opponent's
demands. For example, if you are an airline and your opponent
is booking seats in bulk, he might say: "We can only go ahead if
you give us business class seats," when previously, you had only
been discussing economy seats. If you have spare capacity in
business class, it will not cost you anything to accommodate
the last-minute demand.

3 DEMONSTRATE A REWORKED AGREEMENT
Show your opponent how the demand would have adverse
effects on his business. For example, cutting costs would mean a
lower specification, while bringing forward the delivery date
would jeopardize build quality.

4 SUGGEST RENEGOTIATING PREVIOUS POINTS
You, too, are within your rights to expect him to make some
concessions (a principle called reciprocity). Say: "I appreciate
that the situation has changed, but this moves the goalposts.
I would like to reopen the negotiation on clauses 1, 4, and 7" or
"Okay, so you want to renegotiate the cost. After that, let's
renegotiate the delivery date."

When to walk away

No one but you can decide when it is time to walk away from the deal being negotiated—each case needs to be decided on its merits. Be careful to walk away only as a last resort.

There are times when you consider the negotiation to have reached a conclusion. Notwithstanding deception and other tricks and ploys, only consider leaving the meeting if:

1 You have explained your BATNA (see pp. 62–69) and your intention to use it. You must be prepared to follow your warning through, so if you have no BATNA, or only a weak one, think twice about walking out. Claiming you have a strong BATNA when you don't is a bluff that may not go your way.

2 You feel there is nothing to be lost. Leaving, in this scenario, constitutes a take-it-or-leave-it ultimatum in an attempt to jump-start the negotiation. If you believe there is an agreement to be reached but your opponent is failing to help find that agreement, you may consider throwing down this challenge.

BEFORE YOU ACT, THINK ABOUT THESE QUESTIONS. IF YOUR ANSWERS ARE "YES," THEN YOU HAVE A CLEAR CASE FOR LEAVING:

1 "Am I losing out on other business by trying to do business with an opponent who won't reach agreement with me?" There is always an opportunity cost to wasting your time.

2 "Is there someone else I can do business with?" In almost all business situations, except one involving highly experimental products from specialist manufacturers, there is often another supplier or buyer to deal with.

3 "Can I afford to walk away from the deal under discussion?" Unless you are desperate to strike a deal (and there are instances where a bad deal can get you the foothold you need), and subject to the answers to the two questions above, in many cases the answer to this question may be "yes."

When to walk away continued

DON'T:

1 Walk out as a bluff. This often backfires, particularly if your opponent cannot work with your expectations or has his own strong BATNA.

2 Walk out before all possible avenues have been exhausted. Despite your frustrations, make sure all possibilities are considered.

3 Walk out if you really need to find agreement or have no BATNA. By walking out in this situation, you are just shooting yourself in the foot.

4 Walk out in anger. Don't take it personally if the negotiation comes to an end before you reach an agreement, and resist the temptation to tell your opponent exactly what you think of him.

5 Burn your bridges. You don't know when you'll have to deal with your opponent again. Don't end any chance of doing business again with harsh words.

)O:

1 Remain calm and relaxed. Try to remember that this is a business negotiation, not a personal competition. Losing your cool will not make you, your interests, or the company you represent look very good.

2 Leave the door open to allow the negotiation to reopen. This is essential if you have used the take-it-or-leave it approach outlined above. Your opponent has to feel that he can still pick up the phone if he wants to.

3 Hand them your business card so they can contact you again in the future. Although they may well have your details already, this is a symbolic gesture that you are still reaching out to them, despite the breakdown in the talks.

HOW TO LEAVE. SAY:
"Thank you for your time, it's been an interesting discussion, but I feel that there is now nothing in it for either of us."

"I don't think that the way this discussion is progressing is likely to lead to a positive outcome. Anytime you are ready to reopen the negotiation, please call me."

Dealing with a bully

In negotiation terms, a bully is someone who attempts to coerce you into an agreement by using arrogant and threatening behavior. Unfortunately, it is a commonly used tactic.

HERE'S HOW YOU DEAL WITH BULLYING:

1

PREPARE THOROUGHLY FOR THE MEETING
We have already looked at this, but it is particularly relevant if you think that you are going to be put under undue pressure by your opponent. By having the facts at your fingertips, you can be confident that you know exactly what you are talking about and won't be easily derailed during the meeting.

2

KEEP ASKING QUESTIONS
During the meeting, your bully will try to bombard you with facts, figures, assumptions, and generalizations and aggressively expect you to go along with anything he says. Keep asking for evidence of what you're expected to believe—don't take any of it at face value.

3 TAKE BREAKS
This helps diffuse tense situations and allows you time to find out whether the facts that are being presented to you are true. There is no reason why you shouldn't gently make it clear that you will be checking all statements.

4 KEEP CALM
As always, simply reacting to your opponent means you have lost control and therefore cannot influence the negotiation. Trying to fight it will make matters worse and distract you from what needs to be discussed.

5 REPEAT WHAT YOU NEED TO SAY
Most bullies will just ignore your opinion and shout over you. This makes it difficult to be heard, so do not be afraid to repeat yourself. It keeps you focused and keeps the point under discussion in full view.

6 MAKE NO DECISIONS ON THE SPOT
The bully's aim is to get you to agree to something you normally wouldn't. To negate this, make an excuse, such as needing to sleep on his offer. Have some excuses ready before you go into the meeting.

Negating threats

Threats are a part of the power game. They force you to continue to negotiate while making it clear, either explicitly or implicitly, that there will be serious consequences if you do not agree.

SO WHAT SHOULD YOU DO? HERE ARE SOME TIPS:

1

ACKNOWLEDGE THE THREAT
Say that you have understood that there are consequences if you don't reach agreement. Do not let the threat pass unnoticed. Say:

"I understand that you want to look at other contractors to take on this work if I don't agree to your terms."

2

ASK FURTHER QUESTIONS
Asking clarifying questions makes the threat itself the topic of discussion, which is often an uncomfortable place for your opponent to be. Say:

"Are you saying that we are unlikely to reach agreement here, and that this will have a long-term effect on our future business together?"

3

APPEAR UNRUFFLED

We have seen before how not appearing desperate to strike a deal helps you influence the negotiation process, and this is especially true with threats. A threat is usually a tactic to coerce you into an agreement you would not normally make. So do not react to the threat but remain calm and unbothered. The effect of the tactic will be quickly negated. Say:

"You are obviously entitled to discuss the situation with whoever you like. But this does not change my situation, which is ...."

Again, this puts the ball back in your opponent's court.

when things go awry

Dealing with personal attacks

Personal attacks are another form of powerplay. They are designed to bully you into submission by damaging you status and lowering your self-confidence.

THIS IS HOW TO DEAL WITH THEM:

1 IGNORE THE ATTACK

This is vitally important. Engaging in a slandering match will be counterproductive as the negotiation will quickly come to an end. Remember that you are trying to influence the outcome of the discussion, not be led by your opponent. So you must note the attack and what was said, but ignore it. In many cases, not rising to the bait will stop your opponent from launching attacks, because he will see that they have no impact.

2 REFRAME

Very often, a personal attack is an expression of frustration that the problems behind an issue are not being sorted out. So ignore the attack itself and try to address the issue. If your opponent tells you you're just a time-waster with a pathetic budget, reframe. Say:

"I know you've traveled a long way to see me today, and I appreciate that. What would you suggest to be an acceptable ball-park figure for your product given the changing market conditions?"

3

MOVE ON

The temptation to open up old wounds is always there. Resist this. Instead, briefly acknowledge any past wrongs. Say:

"How can we avoid that kind of situation again?" This moves the focus away from the attack and back onto the matter at hand.

4

ENCOURAGE A COMMON PURPOSE

Attacks are usually framed as: "You have deliberately done the opposite of what we agreed," which encourages the reply: "I did no such thing." This is the type of game that mutually beneficial negotiation seeks to avoid—the defending of positions. Instead, try to encourage a feeling that you are both in it together by using "we." Say:

"How can we make sure that mistakes are not made again?"

Dealing with misinformation

Misinformation is a step down from deception, and not always a bold-faced lie. It is a series of small distortions of the truth intended to manipulate you. All negotiators will find themselves using it at some time to gain advantage.

THIS IS HOW TO DEAL WITH IT:

1 QUESTION ANY FACTS AND FIGURES

The facts and figures your opponent is giving you are intended to cast him in the best possible light, or to put you under pressure. Estimates are presented as accurate quotes, percentages are rounded up or down, timetables are narrowed down to the day when your opponent demands something, but rounded up to the week when you want a concession in return. So do not accept figures at face value. Say:

"In the past, we have had the product delivered within two weeks. Why are you telling me a month is your standard time?"

2 RECAP

Recapping involves pausing the discussion every so often to sum up what you are being told. Say:

"Just to be clear, as I understand it, the situation so far is . . . ."

3 MAINTAIN MENTAL CLARITY
Be clear in your own mind what is being said. If you need to, make some notes as you go along. These will deter your opponent from feeding you misinformation because you now have a written record to refer back to.

4 LOOK AT THE DETAILS
Make it clear that you will be checking all facts and figures before signing any agreement. Say:

"I have to get the figures absolutely right on this …"

5 EXPOSE THE MISINFORMATION
Don't be afraid to point out information that doesn't add up. Say: "I can't see how all this adds up," or "Let's get real!" This is a good way to deter your opponent from feeding you any further untruths.

Dealing with stonewalls

A stonewall is at attempt by your opponent to present you with a final position from which he claims he will not move—you are literally met with an immovable object. Often, this is a tactic to get you to agree to what's on the table by simply refusing to negotiate any further.

Stonewalls usually take the form of a one-sided deadline or a take-it-or-leave-it attitude. You will be told: "If we can't reach agreement by Friday, we're going to sign a contract with your competitor," or: "That's it. That's all we're prepared to pay. If you don't like it, we'll have to go elsewhere." In the face of this, you need to find answers that:

1 Stop you from giving in to the stonewall.

2 Buy time so the deal doesn't fall through.

3 Make it possible for your opponent to back down without losing face.

4 Show your opponent that although you can't meet his demands, you are serious about finding a solution.

HESE ARE THE ANSWERS TO TRY:

1

SEE IF IT'S REAL
This is the acid test—will your opponent see his ultimatum through or is he only bluffing? To start with, you probably cannot afford to just dismiss his stonewall, so a more subtle approach is needed. Start by asking questions. For example, your opponent tells you that the deal has to be done by Friday or it's all off. You know that you are one of several suppliers involved in the deal. Ask:

"I take it then that your other suppliers are contracted and ready to start production?"

Or make a delay sound like a good deal to them:

"Judging by your delivery requirements, it would seem to be a better idea to synchronize delivery with the other suppliers, who I know are not contracted yet."

Dealing with stonewalls continued

2 POINT OUT THE OPPORTUNITY COST

All deadlines, particularly short deadlines, are often broken. In fact, the shorter the deadline, the less likely you will be to fulfill it. So state your case. If, for example, you are negotiating a lease on new business premises and you are told that you must sign by Friday or the deal's off, point out the opportunity cost of going back to square one. Say:

"Friday is not possible. If this deal falls through, we will both have to spend a lot more time and money finding new premises and new tenants. Given that we are so close to a deal, it seems pointless to throw it all away now. Let's see what we can do to make sure that doesn't happen."

3 SUGGEST AN ALTERNATIVE
When you say that you can't meet your opponent's demands,
be aware that simply telling him "no" or "can't do that" will not
please him. So have an alternative plan or schedule ready that
will suit both parties. Say:

"Friday is not possible. However, I am meeting with my lawyers
on Monday and will have queries on the lease over to you by
Tuesday. If they are resolved, we can sign on Wednesday."

4 DRIVE FORWARD
If your opponent attempts to stonewall you by saying: "It's
Friday or never!" turn his demand into a wish. You can reply
by saying:

"Yes, I'd love to get this all wrapped by Friday, too! That way we
could all rest over the weekend. However, it looks like that won't
be possible. Why don't we look at the problems we still have to
resolve, and how we're going to do that."

Taking it step-by-step

A step-by-step process involves presenting the issues to be resolved in manageable bite-size chunks, getting agreement on one chunk, and then moving on to the next.

TRY THIS TRIED AND TRUSTED METHOD OF GRADUALLY WORKING TOWARD AGREEMENT:

1 Start with the issue that is easiest for you to agree on. This will get you going, and as we have seen before, getting your opponent to start saying "yes" sets him on the path to agreeing to the next item.

2 Leave larger issues, or more contentious ones, until later in the negotiation. In many cases, this reduces the risk of stalling the negotiation by attempting to get your opponent to agree to a large chunk or to make a difficult decision on a tricky issue.

3 Note the opportunities that come up from your discussions. As you go along, getting agreement on successive steps may open up further avenues for discussion that were not apparent to start with. This may form the basis for brainstorming any later issues and get both parties thinking along the same lines.

4 If an issue is proving to be tricky, ask if you can go ahead with your proposal on that issue as an experiment. If it doesn't work, then agree to shelve it. If it does work, then you can always point out its benefits and make it permanent.

5 As you take each issue step by step, take heart from the ever-growing number of "yes's," and the ever-shrinking number of "no's." If you come to an issue you can't reach agreement on, point out the number of issues you've already agreed on. This perspective reminds your opponent that a "yes" is possible.

Dealing with good cop–bad cop

We've all seen this in the movies. The bad cop threatens the suspect for his confession, while the good cop actually gets him to talk. This type of mind game is designed to pressure you into making what you think is a good deal. In fact, it is just a trick—the chances are it's a bad deal.

HOW TO DEAL WITH IT:

1 You need to spot it. This means that you must go into the meeting having done your homework and knowing that your interests are not so extreme as to be not worth negotiating over. If your opponent will not move on any point, then you know that something is up.

Bear in mind that the good cop–bad cop routine is obvious in police dramas. But your opponents in a business negotiation may speak as quietly and calmly as ever, making the ploy much harder to spot.

Your interests must be founded on the principle of finding a mutually beneficial agreement. So no matter what is being offered or denied, base your decisions on whether this basic tenet is being met. This means that you are using an outside standard to judge what you are being offered, rather than simply choosing between the options in front of you.

As a matter of principle, therefore, you can turn down deals, no matter what tactics are being used against you, that do not live up to this outside standard.

Unreasonable tactics

Like many negotiation difficulties, opponents who adopt unreasonable positions from which they refuse to move are usually trying to trick you into making a concession that you would not ordinarily make.

UNREASONABLE POSITIONS OCCUR IN A VARIETY OF SITUATIONS:

1

PROBLEM: ACTING UNWILLING TO NEGOTIATE
This occurs when one side flatly refuses to negotiate at all. This is often seen when a third party is involved. Two warring colleagues tell each other: "We'll let the boss be the judge of that."

Solution: Do not give in, attempt to appeal to your opponent's better nature, or throw up your hands, exclaiming: "I can't believe you won't listen to reason!" Instead, leave the issues under discussion to one side and ask yourself:

■ What are his fears?
■ What does he think he has to lose by negotiating with you?

Once you start to uncover his interests, you can get to work on assuring him that you want to find a mutually beneficial agreement.

2

PROBLEM: MAKING UNREASONABLE DEMANDS
This occurs when your opponent apparently agrees to
something but attaches too many strings and then places the
blame on you. For example, your opponent agrees to a price for
your product but wants delivery before you can manufacture
the goods. He is using his unreasonable position as a lever to
get the best possible delivery date.

Solution: Do not give in. Clearly, the deal cannot go ahead. Ask
why your opponent is making such a demand. Bringing it out
into the open often helps the demand melt away—no one
wants to look as if he is the one being unreasonable. If you
reach an impasse, say:

"I'm finding this very frustrating. I cannot see what is leading
you to make demands that I cannot meet. I think we should
take a break and then see if it is possible to resolve this. If not,
then I cannot see how we can continue."

Unreasonable tactics continued

3 PROBLEM: GIVING WITH ONE HAND, TAKING BACK WITH THE OTHER
Your opponent may want to appear as if he is making all the
concessions, but as he agrees to each point, he demands more
in return. In effect, the number of concessions he is making is
greatly reduced, sometimes to the point where he's not giving
anything away at all.

Solution: Do not give in to the tactic. It is designed to:

■ Make sure that you end up with as little as possible.
■ Hurry you into making an agreement before your opponent
  has the chance to make any more demands.

As always, openly acknowledging the tactic, and not reacting to
it, is the best policy. So you can:

■ Suggest that both parties reconsider how they want the
  negotiation to proceed.
■ Make it clear that it will be very difficult to find a mutually
  beneficial agreement if the tactic continues to be used.

4

PROBLEM: EXPLOITING YOUR VULNERABILITIES
Your opponent may know your vulnerabilities and seek to
exploit them to gain the upper hand.
For example, in a negotiation over the purchase of commercial
property, your opponent may have found out that the mortgage
deal carries a low rate of interest but that this rate is only
available for a limited time, putting you under pressure to close
the deal quickly. Your opponent may ask that you agree to extra
concessions or he will deliberately delay the negotiation until
after your loan rate rises.

Solution: Do not give in. Instead, bring the tactic out into the
open and clearly say that you are unwilling to entertain it. A
strong BATNA and a willingness to use it is very useful here.
Your BATNA could be:

■ You have seen other properties and are negotiating with
   other vendors.
■ Any delay on the part of your opponent may result in the
   complete collapse of the current deal.

The power of precedent

A favorite negotiating tactic is the appeal to precedent, that is, your opponent quotes previous examples of behavior or price and uses this as a basis for making a demand.

Precedent is usually found in the following places:

■ **Previous written agreements**
Your opponent may use old contracts or emails, letters, faxes, or memos to back up his demand.

■ **Previous experience**
Your opponent may claim that because something was done one way in the past, this should be the way to proceed in the future.

■ **Comparison**
Your opponent finds out that you have made certain concessions to another client. Why can't he have the same?

■ **The spirit of the agreement**
Your opponent may claim what he is asking for is in the spirit of the agreement.

■ **Industry standard**
Your opponent tells you that his demand is a standard one for the industry you are working in.

HOW DO DEAL WITH IT:

1 Claim that your negotiation must be decided on its own merits and that what has been agreed to in the past has no bearing on what is being decided here and now.

2 Claim that the precedent is out of date. Contractual terms are now anachronistic, and what was relevant in the past is no longer relevant today.

3 Claim that the industry has moved on. Changes in manufacturing or logistics have led to a change in industry standards.

4 Claim that previous agreements were special arrangements, applicable only in one situation.

5 Claim that what you are offering as a package already meets your opponent's interests. This attempts to diminish the importance of precedent.

Dealing with experts

In negotiations involving a high degree of technical complexity, experts are
brought in under the guise of providing technical advice. But their main
purpose is to undermine your arguments, while suggesting that their own
side's ideas are the best way to go.

HOW TO NEGATE EXPERT INFLUENCE:

1 DO YOUR HOMEWORK
Make sure that you know who is going to be at the negotiating
table. If your opponent says he is bringing an expert, bring one of
your own. They will tend to cancel each other out, leaving you to
negotiate the commercial aspects of the deal with your opponent.

2 SIDELINE THE EXPERT
If your opponent brings an expert to the meeting without
forewarning, sideline him by asking him to write down his
concerns, promising to relay them back to your own experts for
an answer at a later date. Do not enter into a technical
conversation with him or negotiate with him at all. Make it
clear that technical considerations are beyond your scope. Then
return to dealing with the commercial aspects of the deal.

3 ASK FOR PROOF
This means asking the expert to provide copies of his reports, data, or research so you can establish his expertise. You are entitled to ask for this kind of documentary evidence, but don't ask for it in a way that makes you sound like you don't believe his credentials are sound.

4 NAME DROP
If you are already supplying one company with technically appropriate products or services, why not let your opponent know this? If what you are producing is good enough for one company, it will serve as a useful precedent that you can serve your opponent's needs as well.

Covering old ground

Going over the same old points during a negotiation is designed to grind you down. This could be designed to panic you into making a concession you would not ordinarily make. Or, your opponent may have a genuine concern about something to which you already agreed.

EITHER WAY, YOUR STRATEGY SHOULD BE:

1 Do not reopen the negotiation on the contentious point. This is exactly what your opponent wants you to do. By doing so, you will set a dangerous precedent for the other issues in your negotiation. What you agreed upon was good enough earlier, so, all things being equal, have the courage of your convictions to convince him that he is doing the right thing.

2 Ask questions. Whether your opponent is using the "broken record" tactic or has a real concern, you must uncover the problem. Ask yourself:

"Is my opponent clear on what he wants?" and "What can I say that will fix the problem?"

In a negotiation over the rental of commercial premises, the point that gets reopened might be price. So:

- Explain that if your opponent wants a cheaper price, he might want to consider opening a smaller/less prestigious store.
- Explain the benefits of the current location, that this will benefit his business and that the cost is genuinely worth it.

This moves him away from the negative issue of cost, and onto the positive issues of growing a retail business.

When a difficult situation arises

These are the twenty steps you should take whenever a difficult situation arises. Remind yourself that when things are going wrong, you should:

■ Remain calm

■ Try to work out whether your opponent's concerns are genuine, or if you are the victim of a ploy

■ Ask questions to uncover unmet interests and the reasons behind problems

■ Base your arguments on the principle of mutual gain

■ State the opportunity cost to your opponent of not doing business

■ Consider the opportunity cost to yourself of not doing business

■ Take a break, either to lower the temperature or to work out your next move

■ Not rush into any on-the-spot decision

■ Not appear desperate to reach agreement

■ Not lock horns

▪ Reframe the issue

▪ Move away from contentious issues and onto ones where "yes" is likely to be the answer

▪ Discuss contentious issues when you can show how far you have come and how close you are to agreement

▪ Acknowledge emotions as genuine and expected

▪ Not walk away unless every avenue has been explored

▪ Always leave the door open if you walk away

▪ Not be overawed by demonstrations of power

▪ Not force your opponent to defend his position

▪ Break the negotiation up into bite-size chunks

▪ Listen actively

Index